A refreshingly easy-to-read book created by professionals with a wealth of knowledge. Practical information for those coping with the day-to-day realities of aging. A real asset to baby boomers and their parents.
   –Robin Mayrl, MSSW
   Former Director, Milwaukee County Department on Aging

An excellent resource for those planning for the latter part of their lives. The authors demonstrate genuine concern for these important issues.
   –Glenn Jonas, CEO
   RF Technologies—Manufacturers of the Code Alert® Systems

What a terrific resource! Clear and engaging, it offers practical instructions and sensitive advice. This eminently useful book should be required reading for older adults and those who care about them.
   –Rabbi David B. Cohen
   Congregation Sinai, Milwaukee, Wisconsin

A Planning Guide for Seniors and Their Families

Phyllis Mensh Brostoff, ACSW, CISW

Matt Furno, NHA

John A. Herbers, JD

Paula H. Hogan, CFP, CFA

Steven J. Koppel, CLU, ChFC

Foreword by
Hannah Rosenthal
Regional Director, U.S. Department of Health and Human Services

ELTON-WOLF PUBLISHING

Milwaukee • Seattle • Vancouver, B.C. • Los Angeles • Portland • Denver

Copyright © 2000 Phyllis Mensh Brostoff, Matt Furno,
John A. Herbers, Paula H. Hogan, and Steven J. Koppel

All rights reserved.

Cover Design and Art by Shelby Keefe
Text Design by Georgene Schreiner
Edited by Carolyn Kott Washburne
Index by Carol Roberts
All photos, unless otherwise indicated, are by *Photography by Jacquie*
OldTalk: New Conversations is a registered trademark of OldTalk LLC

No part of this publication may be reproduced, or utilized in any form or by any means, electronic or mechanical, including photocopying and recording, or by any information storage and retrieval system, without permission in writing from the authors.

04   03   02   01   00   5   4   3   2   1

ISBN 1-58619-050-4
Library of Congress Catalog Card Number: 99-68365

First Printing January 2000
Printed in the United States of America

Published by Elton-Wolf Publishing
Milwaukee, Wisconsin

ELTON-WOLF PUBLISHING

5630 N. Lake Drive, Milwaukee, WI 53217
414-906-0600 • e-mail:spittelman@elton-wolf.com
Milwaukee • Seattle • Vancouver, B.C. • Los Angeles • Portland • Denver

This book is dedicated to those who are growing older…

and those who love and care for them.

TABLE OF CONTENTS

FOREWORD ix
    Hannah Rosenthal, Regional Director
    U.S. Department of Health and Human Services

INTRODUCTION 1

CHAPTER ONE 5
Planning for a Financially Comfortable Retirement
    by Paula H. Hogan, CFP, CFA

CHAPTER TWO 29
Estate and Tax Planning
    by John A. Herbers, JD

CHAPTER THREE 47
Long-Term Care Insurance—The New Financial Necessity
    by Steven J. Koppel, CLU, ChFC

CHAPTER FOUR 67
Getting the Care You Need When You Live at Home
    by Phyllis Mensh Brostoff, ACSW, CISW

CHAPTER FIVE 81
Choosing Your New Home: Retirement/Senior Housing
    by Matt Furno, NHA

POSTSCRIPT FROM THE AUTHORS 105

AUTHOR PROFILES 107

INDEX 110

FOREWORD

Americans today are living longer and healthier lives than ever before. Yet not much in our culture prepares us for our own longevity.

OldTalk: New Conversations is designed to facilitate conversations about the issues we will all face in the latter part of our lives. Written by five professionals who specialize in issues of pre- and postretirement, *OldTalk: New Conversations* offers guidelines for the financial, legal, medical, and lifestyle transitions of later life. The information presented will empower us and our loved ones to make informed decisions about these transitions.

Although aging is not a topic that any of us deals with easily, dealing with it *well* can make all the difference. The keys to enjoying later life are understanding and planning for what lies ahead. It is never too late—or too soon—to begin. Being prepared and talking frankly can help ensure that as you age, you are enjoying the best quality of life possible.

We at the Department of Health and Human Services believe that the concepts of self-preparation and personal responsibility are crucial to aging well.

I hope that *OldTalk: New Conversations* will serve as a guide to help you begin the important process of planning for the future today to ensure a more comfortable tomorrow.

Hannah Rosenthal, Regional Director
U.S. Department of Health and Human Services

INTRODUCTION

◆

Welcome to

OldTalk, New Conversations

A Planning Guide for Seniors and their Families

OldTalk:New Conversations explores questions that we are all facing, or will face sooner or later: the questions of what to do as we get old, or as our loved ones get old. This book focuses on questions that need to be asked, information that needs to be shared, and decisions that need to be made. Once the questions are asked, we can begin to answer them. But until we know what to ask, we are simply trudging along a path on our journey without any sense of our destination or the alternate routes we might use.

This book will help you deal with many of the day-to-day realities of caring for older people. It is written for the layperson and helps identify the sorts of information that you will need to gather. This information will then let you, the reader, help yourself and your loved ones as you confront and deal with the aging process.

Old Talk *New Conversations*

We decided to write this book partly because we face these issues daily in our professional lives, and partly because we are beginning to face these questions in our personal lives as well. As we write this book, several of the authors are struggling with many of the issues discussed here in relation to their parents. No one single author has all of the answers, and even as a group the solutions that we develop for ourselves and our families are not always perfect. However, by sharing information among ourselves, we are able to make sure that all the important issues are addressed and all the right questions are asked.

OldTalk:New Conversations begins with a chapter on the financial aspects of growing older. Paula Hogan explores the financial implications of retirement and postretirement living. She describes how we must transition from income-earners and asset-accumulators to income-spenders and asset-liquidators. Her message is that we have to change our financial mindset in order to adjust to the financial realities of growing older. Paula is a financial planner whose firm provides comprehensive, fee-only financial planning and portfolio management services.

John Herbers, an attorney, describes the legal structures that most people use in their estate planning. These legal structures include the typical estate-planning process of developing a will and trust to transfer assets after death and also the just-as-important issues of dealing with our affairs in the event of a disability. John's chapter also describes briefly some of the basic tax implications of transferring assets to our loved ones, both during lifetime and after death.

Steve Koppel, a life insurance Chartered Life Underwriter, looks at long-term care insurance as a method of payment for the

INTRODUCTION

costs of long-term healthcare. Given the escalating costs of healthcare and the diminishing ability of the government to cover these costs, long-term care insurance and other private-pay alternatives offer viable solutions in many situations.

Phyllis Mensh Brostoff's chapter is about home care options. Phyllis explores the alternatives available to people who require increasing personal assistance in order to remain in their own homes. Phyllis is a geriatric social worker whose agency provides professional care evaluation and monitoring services.

Finally, Matt Furno, the President/CEO of a senior living community, explores the purposes and functions of senior living. He describes the issues that need to be addressed in selecting which level of care and which facility to use.

Our purpose in writing this book is to share information—basic information—about getting old. We keep the discussion fairly general and nontechnical because we want to establish a basic framework of information that you can use as the foundation for further discussions with your loved ones. We want to start slowly and allow you to gather momentum in your planning as you go at your own pace.

All of the authors work in Wisconsin, and so the book includes some references to specific situations we see here and terminology that is unique to our state. However, the general themes are consistent across the country as we enter the new millennium.

This book is not a panacea for us and our families and friends as we get older. It is not an exhaustive attempt to document the aging process or to address all of the issues that can and must be faced as we and our loved ones grow old. It is an attempt to begin the conversation between those people who are growing

Old Talk *New Conversations*

older and those who love and care for them. It is a book to stimulate this absolutely necessary conversation between spouses, between friends, and between parents and children as we all struggle with the process of getting old.

In this book we do not shrink from the word "old." Many euphemisms for "old" abound in popular jargon, such as "elder," "senior," and "golden." We use "old" because we are dealing frankly with the issues that people face as they age.

We hope that you will use this book and its chapters as a springboard for discussions with your doctors, care providers, professional advisors, and, most importantly, with your families and loved ones. In time these conversations will no longer be about getting and being old, but about life.

CHAPTER ONE

PLANNING FOR A FINANCIALLY COMFORTABLE RETIREMENT

BY PAULA H. HOGAN, CFP, CFA

Getting Oriented

You have reached retirement age with some personal wealth and good health. Now what? The old patterns of living no longer apply. The pressures of work and family-raising are over. Now it's time for you. But what does that mean? It's a new situation, and you have a lot of questions:

- How much can I safely spend each year and not run out of money?
- How will I keep busy? What will I do all day?
- How do I handle medical and custodial care issues for myself—and my spouse?
- How much will my children inherit—and do I give them some of that inheritance now?
- When do I think about moving out of my home—and where would I go?
- What if something happens and I become incapacitated? Would I be safe?

Old Talk *New Conversations*

These are daunting questions. Fortunately, however, you're not supposed to have all the answers right away. You've never been retired before, and not much in our culture really prepares people for modern retirement, as the longevity statistics reveal. In the beginning of this century life expectancy in our country was about 47 years. Now life expectancy at birth is about 80 years for women and about 73 years for men. It is no wonder we're all a little disoriented; the amount of time we spend in adulthood has more than doubled in the last century. Retirement as we know it is a fairly new phenomenon. We are on new ground. So take some time to get oriented, and draw up a map for where you are headed.

Your map to a financially secure retirement starts with the **balance sheet**. This snapshot of your finances provides a wealth of information about what you have going for you and where you are vulnerable. (See the sample balance sheet on pages 8 and 9.)

The asset section of the balance sheet is the list of what you own, including liquid assets (the assets used for day-to-day expenses), investment accounts (the assets that support future expenses), and personal property (the nonfinancial part of your wealth).

Liquid Assets. These include daily checking accounts and emergency reserves, the first line of defense against financial hardship. Financial advisors typically recommend having from three to six months of living expenses in a money market or other liquid account, for example, a very short-term bond fund. (Liquid assets are assets that can be readily converted to cash with no loss of value. Certificates of Deposit are not good assets for emergency reserves because you usually have to pay a penalty to get cash before the maturity date.) If you are in a high tax bracket, use a tax-exempt account for emergency reserves in order to maximize the after-tax return. You are in a high tax bracket if your taxable income (Line 37 of the your 1999 1040 tax return) exceeds $104,050 if you file jointly, or $62,450 if you file singly.

Investment Accounts. These are typically held for long periods and are key to your future standard of living. To be successful, they must grow over time and be well managed. Keeping taxes minimized is also an important consideration for investment accounts.

Personal Property. This is listed separately to honor its unavailability to pay bills today but still to recognize it as an important form of wealth. At financial turning points you might convert personal-use assets into financial wealth.

Liabilities. The liability section of the balance sheet is the list of what you owe. In the real world it can be hard to manage debt. But the goal, especially in retirement, is to be debt free so that retirement income is completely available for daily expenses. If you reach retirement with some debt still remaining, take a good look at the pros and cons, and the feasibility of paying the debt off completely. Remember that paying down a dollar of debt is comparable to directing a dollar to an investment with an immediate, pretax return approximately equal to the interest rate on the debt.

OldTalk *New Conversations*

SAMPLE BALANCE SHEET
A snapshot of your financial strengths and weaknesses

Hogan Financial Management

ASSETS
(What you own)

LIQUID ASSETS *(Your cushion for day-to-day expenses)*

    Checking Accounts *(Use usual month-end balance.)* _____ LQ

    Savings / Money Market Accounts _____ LQ
    (Have at least 3-6 months living expenses here.)

    Cash Surrender Value Life Insurance _____ LQ
    (It's often a good idea to pay off insurance loan balances.)

    TOTAL LIQUID ASSETS *(Add LQs.)* _____ **A**
    (Your first defense against financial misfortune)

INVESTMENT ACCOUNTS *(A key determinant of your future standard of living)*

    Taxable Accounts (That is, not tax-sheltered retirement accounts)

        Certificates of Deposit *(List all of them!)* _____ F

        Taxable Bonds or Bond Funds _____ F
        (Traditional role in portfolio is to decrease volatility.)

        Stocks _____ F
        (High-potential return in exchange for year-to-year volatility)

        Mutual Funds _____ F
        (Usually a mixture of stocks, bonds, and CD-like investments)

        Other *(e.g. Limited partnerships, closely held business interests)* _____ F

    Tax-Sheltered Retirement Accounts

        IRA – Ordinary _____ F

        IRA – Roth _____ F

        Work-Related Accounts _____ F

        SEP-IRAs _____ F
            (From self-employment earnings)

        401(k), Profit Sharing _____ F
            (Retirement accounts from for-profit employers)

        403(b) Accounts _____ F
            (Retirement accounts from nonprofit employers)

        Value of Vested Pension Benefit _____ F
            (Your benefits office has this number.)

        Annuities *(Not IRAs)* _____ F

    TOTAL INVESTMENT ACCOUNTS *(Add Fs.)* _____ **B**

PERSONAL PROPERTY
(These assets affect your day-to-day standard of living and, to a limited extent, your future standard of living. They can be hard to value. Use low estimates.)

Residence	_____	P
Vacation Home	_____	P
Special Collections *(Use the insured value.)*	_____	P
Personal Property	_____	P
(Useful estimate: make this number 50% of the Residence value.)		

TOTAL PERSONAL PROPERTY *(Add Ps.)* _____ **C**

TOTAL ASSETS *(Add A, B, and C.)* _____ **I**
(What you have going for you)

LIABILITIES
(What you owe)

Credit Card *(Enter zero if paid in full each month— and do pay in full each month.)*	_____	L
Mortgage *(Everything gets easier with completed mortgage payments.)*	_____	L
Gifts Promised to Family Members *(Are these commitments or intentions?)*	_____	L
Charitable Pledges *(Are these commitments or intentions?)*	_____	L

TOTAL LIABILITIES *(Add Ls.)* _____ **II**
(What you have going against you)

NET WORTH
(It's the difference between what you own—ASSETS and what you owe—LIABILITIES.)

*(Subtract **II** from **I**.)* _____

OldTalk New Conversations

Note: Don't forget loans on insurance policies. These loans are often particularly good candidates for repayment, since the interest rate earned by whole life policies, especially when no policy loan is in place, is often attractive and tax-protected.

If your investment accounts are not sufficient to pay off all debt, then shift to an alternate strategy. For example, if there is no way you can pay off your home mortgage in full and still have money left over for daily expenses, then work with the lender to make the mandatory payment as low as possible and also fixed in nature. Do what you can to minimize mandatory debt payments. By minimizing fixed obligations, you free up income for the other expenses of daily living.

You can draw up a balance sheet for yourself in about half an hour using the sample balance sheet as a model. Don't worry about getting the perfect numbers; just use the best available estimates. Add up all of your assets and all of your liabilities. Subtract liabilities from assets to get your **net worth**, a key measure of financial strength.

Take a look at the components of your net worth. Do you have cash reserves equal to at least three months' living expenses? Do you have debt that could be paid off? Are your investment accounts well-diversified and positioned for prudent growth? Is personal property appropriate for your lifestyle and your level of wealth?

The second critical part of your map to a financially comfortable retirement is the **cash flow** statement. This report provides a "movie" of cash flowing in and out over a specific period of time, typically a year. A cash flow statement can be easily created for your own finances.

First, list each income source and its annual amount. (See sample cash flow statement.) Be sure to use realistic estimates. Review each income source. How secure is each item? How long will it last? Is income well diversified by source? How well will each income stream keep up with inflation?

Income that is fixed as a level payment, rather than going up each year with inflation, will shrink dramatically in value over time. For example, with an inflation rate of 4.5 percent, the sum of purchases you could make with a particular fixed level of income will halve over the course of 15 years. If inflation continues at 4.5 percent for another 15 years, the standard of living attainable with that original fixed income would fall to a quarter of the original amount. Inflation is a serious threat to anyone living on a fixed income for more than a short period of time.

In retirement there is a particular challenge to defining income: how do you convert portfolio wealth into an income stream? In other words, how much can you draw from investment accounts each year and not outlive your money? Some people define portfolio income as interest and dividends. But this definition can be dangerously misleading. Interest and dividends are only one component of the wealth generated by investment assets. Capital gains (or losses) is the other. Spending one and ignoring the other can result in your inadvertently spending either too little or too much.

OldTalk *New Conversations*

SAMPLE CASH FLOW STATEMENT
A movie of your day-to-day expenses

Hogan
Financial
Management

INCOME
(Money coming in—Use low estimates.)

EARNED INCOME _____ I

INVESTMENT INCOME

Financial (Traditionally defined as interest and dividends, but more sensibly and prudently defined as some conservative annual percentage of your portfolio, e.g. 3-5%.) _____ I

Rental (After all expenses, including reserves for maintenance) _____ I

SOCIAL SECURITY INCOME
(Surviving spouse gets the higher of his/her payment or his/her deceased spouse's payment.) _____ I

PENSION INCOME _____ I
(Does it go up with inflation? What goes to the surviving spouse?)

DEFERRED COMPENSATION (How long does it last?) _____ I

FAMILY GIFTS/SUPPORT PAYMENTS _____ I
(What you're actually getting. How long will they last?)

TOTAL INCOME (Add Is.) _____ 1
(Be sure to live within this number. HINT: If debt is rising or savings declining, you're not living within your income.)

EXPENSES
(Money going out—Use high estimates.)

FIXED (Even if you go to a desert island for a year, you still have to pay these expenses.)

HOME
- Mortgage Interest & Principal _____ FE
- Property Insurance _____ FE
- Condo Fees _____ FE
- Property Taxes _____ FE

INSURANCE
- Health _____ FE
- Unreimbursed Health Expenses _____ FE
  (Prescription drugs are expensive.)
- Long-Term Care (Buy sooner rather than later.) _____ FE
- Life _____ FE
- Property—Car _____ FE
- Personal Liability _____ FE

FAMILY GIFTS/SUPPORT PAYMENTS _____ FE

TAXES
   Federal _____ FE
   State _____ FE
   Local _____ FE

OTHER
   Charitable Commitments _____ FE
   Club Fees _____ FE
   Professional Fees _____ FE

SAVINGS *(Usually stops in retirement)* _____ FE

TOTAL FIXED *(Add FEs.)* _____ **2**
(Life is a lot easier if you keep this number low.)

FUNDS AVAILABLE FOR DAILY LIVING
(Subtract 2 from 1.) _____ **3**

VARIABLE EXPENSES
   Clothing & Personal Grooming _____ VE
   Car Maintenance & Gasoline _____ VE
   Home & Yard Maintenance _____ VE
   Utilities _____ VE
   Travel _____ VE
   Books & Subscriptions _____ VE
   Charity & Gifts _____ VE
   Entertainment _____ VE
   Food _____ VE
   Other _____ VE

TOTAL VARIABLE EXPENSES *(Add VEs.)* _____ **4**

INCOME MINUS EXPENSES *(Subtract 2 and 4 from 1.)* _____
(If this number is not positive, you're not making it.)

Old Talk New Conversations

An alternative to spending interest and dividend payments is to think of your portfolio as a charitable foundation, an organization meant to live and generate cash payments forever. If funds are invested in a mixture of stocks, bonds, and money market instruments, you can safely withdraw 3-5 percent of your whole portfolio each year and still live forever, because 3-5 percent is well within a reasonable estimate of long-term annual expected portfolio return. Pick a specific targeted percentage that works for your situation and transfer that percentage of your portfolio out of investment accounts and into daily bank accounts once each year.

By having a targeted withdrawal rate, you set yourself a signpost indicating how much you can spend each year and not dip into capital. If you never dip into capital, you can live forever. If you routinely spend capital, you risk outliving your money and, as the saying goes, having to die on time.

Most investors find it reassuring to set their routine standard of living within their default withdrawal rate, and, further, to set a withdrawal rate that, everything else being equal, is somewhat low early in retirement and then higher in old age. In this way when special opportunities or family emergencies arise, you can afford to acknowledge the high value of the expenditure as well as the fact that none of us lives forever, and go ahead with the highly valued expenditure. Also, in years when the market soars ahead, many investors consider taking less than the default withdrawal rate. Then, when the market falls, they will be better able to take a little more than indicated by the default withdrawal rate and so keep their daily budget on a more even keel.

Investment Note: In general, the higher the component of stocks in your portfolio, the higher the reasonable withdrawal rate. Over the long term stocks have offered a substantially higher rate of return than other investments. But the cost of this higher return is much higher year-to-year volatility. For this reason many investors gradually pull back their stock allocation from the 55-85 percent stock allocations that are typical for portfolios in the preretirement accumulation phase to somewhere in the 30-55 percent range in retirement. A lower stock allocation muffles volatility but also long-term returns. Consequently, the more an investor pulls back to a lower stock allocation, the more appropriate it is to pull back the targeted withdrawal rate, for example toward the 3-4 percent range. In contrast, investors who have more portfolio wealth than they need for themselves can afford, if they choose, to target a very high stock allocation and so, in essence, invest the portfolio more for heirs than for themselves.

Tax-Planning Note: In the year after you turn 70½, under current tax law, your retirement investment accounts may become subject to mandatory withdrawal requirements. Deciding what calculation method to use has important implications for long-term tax planning and is also irrevocable once payments begin. For this reason prudent investors typically consult with their financial advisor, accountant, and/or attorney before making the first mandatory withdrawal, which usually occurs in the year the investor turns 70½. With respect to financial planning, however, remember that these mandatory withdrawals can be either spent or reinvested in your taxable portfolio accounts, depending on your targeted portfolio withdrawal.

Next, make a list of expenses. Look at each expense. Can any item be reduced? Does each item make sense for you? Is each important expense included? You'll note that expenses in retirement are somewhat different than preretirement expenses. In cash flow statements for retired persons, instead of mortgage payments and regular savings, it's much more common to see long-term care insurance premiums and condominium fees. Your financial statements reflect your situation. In retirement the financial issues shift from accumulating wealth to ensuring safety from incapacity and inflation.

Health Insurance Note: In retirement a major fixed expense is healthcare, and especially prescription drugs. As a retiree be ready for change in this important area as insurers continue to control costs and shift expense to the insured. Some retirees are fortunate to be covered in retirement by the group plan of their former employer, but the continuation of such coverage over the long term is not certain. Become familiar with the terms of your coverage. For example, some policies do not offer coverage when you are traveling abroad. Some health plans don't offer coverage if you live out-of-area for more than a certain period of time each year. Checking the financial strength of your health plan is also prudent; check with a financial rating service such as Weiss Ratings (800-289-9222) or A.M. Best (www.ambest.com).

Cash Flow Note: Especially for married couples who are trying to coordinate expenses, it is difficult, if not impossible, to get an accurate estimate of daily discretionary spending by tracking each expenditure. So give yourself a break. Forget about trying to track daily discretionary expenses. Instead, arrange to have all fixed expenses paid (or set aside in a reserve account) immediately after income is received. Then standardize cash withdrawals to some regular monthly amount, minimize check writing, and use just one major credit card for discretionary expenses. Then you can develop an estimate of how high your credit card bill can safely be each month. As long as the credit card bill comes in under target, if fixed expenses are accurately estimated and you are enjoying daily life, then you've met your financial goals.

In general, try hard to live within the budget implied by your cash flow statement. If you find that cash flow is tight, take a fresh look at expenses. Are there any expenses that you can safely reduce? Are there any expenses that, in retrospect and with a better knowledge of your budget, seem high? And finally, take another look at the possibility of earned income. Many retired people work at part-time jobs, some for money and some just to be involved. Sometimes having just a little more income can make a big difference in daily life. As a last resort increase your portfolio withdrawal rate. This is a big decision, but sometimes appropriate. In essence it implies a value decision about the relative importance of spending now versus continuing to save for some unknown, and not even guaranteed, future.

OldTalk New Conversations

By reviewing your balance sheet and cash flow statements, you can get a good idea of what you have going for you and where you are vulnerable financially at this stage of retirement. You can also develop a sense of how much money you can safely spend each year.

Facing Aging Worries: Incapacity

Now take another look at your financial statements and roll the camera forward to a time when you and/or your spouse might become incapacitated and need custodial care. Do you have the resources for this major expense?

The cost for full-time custodial care varies greatly from region to region and from facility to facility. In the Midwest the cost ranges from a low of about $35,000 to a high of $80,000 per year. Paying this amount of money for more than a short time, or for more than one person, would create havoc for most family budgets. How long will you need care? There is some actuarial data about the odds of needing care and the average length of stay, but using the data as an individual is problematic. The actuaries are concerned about a whole group of people, but you are concerned about your own specific family. Do you want to be financially secure on average, or with some higher level of reliability? Remember also that the average-length-of-care data were developed when life expectancy was shorter and modes of care not as advanced as they are now.

This isn't a topic that any of us deals with easily. As most people of retirement age already know, it's hard enough when the health of your own parents begins to fail, but the idea of planning for one's own incapacity is, for most people, literally unspeakable. Nonetheless, the issue is real, and ensuring that your own preferences are carried out is good motivation for dealing with the facts. The facts are that custodial care is expensive and likely to be an issue for you at some point in your life. Perhaps most importantly, if you don't plan where you will live in old age, who will? As anyone who has cared for an older loved one knows, it's a blessing to the family when family members know your preferences and arrangements have been made.

Not surprisingly, given the increase in longevity, there are a growing number of options for where to live in old age. (Chapters Four and Five of this book talk about these issues in more detail.) On either coast retirees are moving into the independent living sections of retirement communities many years earlier than previously. Many excellent facilities already have long waiting lists. And throughout the nation a growing number of businesses are popping up to help people stay in their homes for a longer time, and this trend is likely to continue.

These trends make it prudent for you to look around and begin to think specifically about where you would like to live in old age. For most of us it is no longer the custom to move in with our adult children once we grow old. Visit several retirement communities. Get on a waiting list. Pick a nursing home as a back-up plan in case your preference for either continuing to live at home or for moving into a particular retirement community does not work out as planned. And finally, decide if long-term care insurance makes sense for you. For an increasing portion of the population it does. Long-term care insurance has improved substantially in just the last few years and may well be on its way to becoming fairly standard insurance coverage. If you haven't

Old Talk *New Conversations*

comparison shopped for this insurance coverage recently, it's worth another look. (Chapter Three of this book provides more detailed information on long-term care insurance.)

A useful way to think about long-term care insurance is that in exchange for an annual premium, you get access to a large pot of money that you can use to pay for custodial care, either in your home or in a facility, all on a pretax basis. Usually there is a waiver of premium once full-time care begins and a spousal discount for couples. Also, some portion of the annual premium may be tax deductible. Buying coverage earlier rather than later not only captures a relatively lower premium, it also protects against the possibility of becoming uninsurable. You can buy inflation protection by purchasing an inflation rider that will make the benefits grow, for example, at 5 percent compounded each year. Premiums, however, are fixed in nature and not scheduled to increase from year to year. As a point of reference a 68-year-old purchasing a $100/day, six-year policy with an inflation rider would pay about $2,750/year. In doing so, he gains access to a bucket of money equal to $219,000 (OR $100/day x 365 days/year x 6 years) that will grow at 5 percent/year compounded.

How much coverage to purchase is a judgment call, but most people only insure a portion of the potential custodial care expense. As you decide how much coverage to purchase, remember that most if not all of your income will still be available to contribute to custodial care costs. Also, what you now pay in income taxes would also very likely be at least partially redirected toward custodial costs if you become incapacitated. (Custodial care expenses are tax-deductible medical expenses to the extent that they exceed 7.5 percent of adjusted gross income. In full-time custodial care the result is that funds formerly used for income taxes are in effect often redirected to custodial care costs.) And finally, if you move into an assisted-living or nursing home facility, the proceeds from the sale of your former home will also be available to help pay custodial care costs.

So who should buy long-term care insurance? There are a variety of good candidates, including:

◆ People who can afford to pay for some but not a lot of custodial care with private funds, but who are worried about outliving their money, and/or are concerned that their children's inheritance will be diminished by custodial care costs. If they can't pay premiums out of regular income, these people might pay the premium with cash from the portfolio, not regular income. They view long-term care insurance as portfolio insurance.

◆ Couples where one spouse is unwell and who want to free up personal funds for the spouse with medical problems but still preserve financial security for the healthy spouse.

◆ Executives entering their peak earning years who have adequate disability insurance but not so much disability insurance and/or wealth that they could pay nursing home expenses for themselves and still maintain the family's standard of living. (Of the people in custodial care now, 40 percent are under the age of 65.)

◆ Wealthy people who could afford to pay all custodial care expenses with private funds but who don't want to do so. Precisely because they are wealthy, they are also able to choose to pay long-term care insurance premiums and get the "pop-up" portfolio that long-term care insurance provides to pay custodial care expenses with pretax dollars.

Old Talk New Conversations

- Adult children buying long-term care insurance for their parents as the most cost-effective way to uphold family values.
- Spouses in second marriages who require each other in the prenuptial contract to carry long-term care insurance in order to preserve individual assets for children from a prior marriage.
- And finally, people who look at the custodial care industry and anticipate that managed care trends might shift from healthcare to custodial care, and so purchase long-term care insurance in order to maintain choice.

As these examples make clear, it may be many years before the long-term insurance company is asked to provide benefits. Consequently, and as you will read about in more detail in Chapter Three, purchasing coverage from a strong insurance company is important, as is working with an insurance agent who is specialized in this area. It is also prudent to carefully compare contract language between competing policies as you comparison shop for coverage.

Facing Aging Worries: Inheritances

One of the more common questions posed by retirees to financial advisors is how and when to give financial gifts to adult children. Tax advisors can help determine how much and when to make gifts for tax reasons, but taxes, as parents know best, are only one factor to consider. A further complication is that usually there is no family model for making gifts. After all, the parents of many current retirees did not live long enough or accumulate enough wealth to have developed any useful family patterns for making financial gifts to adult children. Also, they may not have concurred with the view apparently widely held today that parents should offer financial gifts to adult children.

Family gifts can have a powerful ripple effect on family relations. Parents often struggle over such decisions as whether to give gifts only when requested or only when not solicited, or whether to give money with no strings attached or only for a targeted purpose. Whether to make gifts to your child or to your child and that child's spouse, or just to the grandchildren, can also be a troubling decision. Parents also wonder how to treat siblings equitably when the siblings differ greatly from each other. And finally, once a gift program starts, it can be hard to stop. Because of all of these issues, take some time to think through your family's gift strategy.

The anecdotal evidence suggests that gifts work best when three conditions are present:

- The donor is compelled by the sheer pleasure of giving and not for any other reason,
- The donor is not acting contrary to his or her own personal values or financial security, and
- There is sufficiently good communication between the parties so that intentions can be discussed and believed.

Whether or when to make gifts is a highly personal decision that is worthy of reflection and probably also of some family discussion. These issues also lead to consideration of your overall estate plan, which among other tasks provides a vehicle for distributing gifts after your lifetime.

Estate planning is the means by which you ensure that your preferences with respect to both medical and financial affairs are carried out in the event of your death or incapacity. Estate plans typically include a will, sometimes a revocable trust, and also Durable Power of Attorney for both medical and financial affairs.

Old Talk *New Conversations*

Consider getting your estate plan reviewed whenever there is a major change in your personal or financial circumstances, and also whenever there is a major change in estate tax law. (Chapter Two of this book provides detailed information on estate and tax planning.)

When you update your documents, your attorney will need to know your preferences about many important value decisions, including, for example, whom you would choose to speak for you with respect to both medical and financial affairs in the event of your incapacity. (You need a first choice and a backup choice for each area!) Your attorney will also ask you how you would like your estate given away after your death, including charitable bequests, if any, and whether you will leave inheritances outright to your heirs or with some conditions.

It is prudent to work with an attorney specialized in estate planning and to supply your attorney with full information about your finances and your preferences. Once your estate plan is complete, be sure to follow carefully your attorney's recommendations with respect to beneficiary designations on retirement accounts and life insurance policies, and also the titling of various assets. In this way you maximize the chance that your preferences will be carried out.

As part of the estate planning process consider making a map for your heirs that will be helpful to them in the event of your sudden death or incapacity. As the sample **Road Map for Heirs** on pages 26-28 shows, your loved ones need to know the location of important documents, your preferences for death and burial circumstances, and the names and phone numbers of your advisors and physicians.

Developing New Patterns: A Commitment to Yourself

Look around at the people who seem to thrive in retirement versus those who remain adrift. The ones who forge ahead have found ways to branch out into new endeavors that have meaning for them. They often appear to have made a commitment to fitness, both physically and mentally, and often spiritually. They stay connected with the community, whether it's learning e-mail to communicate with the grandchildren, committing to some substantive volunteer work, developing a new hobby, or plunging into an educational endeavor. They have somehow found a way to release themselves from their preretirement identity and to move on to something new. If you listen carefully, the transition into retirement wasn't always easy or smooth. It's a big change, requiring perseverance and effort, and especially patience with yourself and with your partner. Forging on to new territory takes energy and courage, but the rewards are there—and you are the only one who can do it.

In a similar way the transition from early old age into real old age is a transition that also takes energy and courage for the whole family. You are once again forging new ground, with few useful role models and a lot of trepidation. But once again, it is possible to plan ahead, and being prepared can make all the difference.

Old Talk *New Conversations*

ROAD MAP FOR HEIRS

Hogan Financial Management

In the event of your sudden death or incapacity, your heirs need a map of your personal affairs. Use the following list as a starting point. Keep it up to date and be sure your heirs have a current copy.

Your Home

Security:
Who has an extra key? Where is an extra key hidden?
How does one turn off the security system?

Employees:
Who works for you?
On what schedule and for what compensation?

Friends/Neighbors:
Who knows you and watches out for you?
Who would help in the event of an emergency?

Local Police:
What are the emergency and nonemergency phone numbers?

Financial Records:
Where are your financial records kept within your home?
If you use a home computer, where is a list of your computer passwords?
Where are original copies of your will, trusts, and Durable Powers of Attorney?
Where is your safe deposit box, and where do you keep the key?

Driving Directions:
If you have moved away from the home where you lived previously, what are the driving directions to your house, e.g. from the nearest airport?

ROAD MAP FOR HEIRS

Your Healthcare

Primary Physician—Name and phone number.

Specialist Physician(s)—Names and phone numbers.

Health Insurance—Company, phone, identification numbers.

Prescription Medicines—List them.

Pharmacy—Name, address, and phone number.
   Where do you keep prescription medicines in your home?

Preferred Hospital:

Preferred Nursing Home:

Preferred Retirement Community:

Preferred Funeral Home:

Your Advisors

Whom would you like your heirs to contact in the event of a major incapacity or death? Give full names and phone numbers and, where applicable, the name of the firm.

Attorney

Priest/Rabbi/Minister

Social Worker or Retirement Community Ombudsman

Financial Advisor

Accountant

Insurance Agent

Banker

Broker

Veterinarian

Friends/Colleagues/Family Members

Old Talk New Conversations

ROAD MAP FOR HEIRS

Prearrangements

Custodial Care:
Have you made prearrangements for custodial care?
  If so, where are the details of these prearrangements written?
Have you purchased long-term care insurance?
  If so, from what company? Where do you keep the policy?

Postmortem Preferences:
Have you prearranged for postmortem preferences?
  If so, where are the details of these prearrangements written?
Would you like your body to be cremated, buried, entombed, embalmed, donated to science?
Do you intend to make an organ donation?
Have you purchased a burial plot? A headstone?
Have you chosen a funeral home?
  If so, where are the details of these prearrangements written?

Data for Death Certificate—for Both Husband and Wife:
Full Legal Name
Social Security Number
Date of Birth
Date of Death
Birthplace
Mother's Full Maiden Name
Father's Full Name
Military Veteran: Yes or No?
Race
Occupation & Highest Level of Education
Full Birth Name of Surviving Spouse, if applicable

CHAPTER TWO

ESTATE AND TAX PLANNING

BY JOHN A. HERBERS, JD

Estate Planning

Estate planning includes transferring your assets to your beneficiaries after your death, as well as providing for your financial and medical care in the event of your disability during your lifetime. This chapter will focus on transferring your property after your death and managing your affairs in the event of your disability. Later in this chapter we will deal with the tax consequences of transferring your property during your lifetime and after your death.

Planning for Disability

There are two fundamental issues that should be addressed when planning for disability: (a) creating the legal structure to allow for someone else to manage your affairs on your behalf; and (b) financing the cost of your care. (The financing alternatives are discussed in Chapters One and Three of this book.) The legal structure for managing your affairs further breaks down between managing your business and financial affairs and managing your personal and medical care.

Legal Guardianship. Legal guardianship will apply to you in the event of a finding of your legal incompetence, whether by reason of developmental disability, infirmities of aging, accident, illness, or other cause. A person under legal guardianship is called a **ward**. Separate guardianships can be established for financial and personal matters (called guardianship of the estate and guardianship of the person, respectively), or a unified guardianship can be established to cover all of these issues. A guardian is appointed by the court and is accountable to the court. The court proceeding to obtain guardianship involves doctors, lawyers, social workers, and the inevitable costs and loss of privacy that go along with involving all of these other people in your care and financial decisions. A guardianship typically ends upon death of the ward, at which time the guardian is accountable to the personal representative of the estate of the deceased ward.

Conservatorship. An alternative to guardianship of the estate is conservatorship. Conservatorship allows for management of a person's financial affairs but without a finding of legal incompetence. Conservatorships are voluntary in that the ward must request the court to appoint a conservator. Guardianships are involuntary in that the court can establish a guardianship even over the objection of the ward. A conservator is accountable to the court during the ward's lifetime, and to the deceased ward's personal representative after the ward's death.

Durable Power of Attorney. A Durable Power of Attorney is a document that designates an **attorney-in-fact** to handle all or a specified number of financial and business matters of the **principal**. The authority of the attorney-in-fact can come into existence immediately and continue during the principal's incapacity. As an alternative, the authority of the attorney-in-fact can "spring" into existence only in the event of the principal's disability. Married couples will often select the first alternative when designating each other as attorney-in-fact so that either spouse can handle any financial matter for both spouses. A single person or surviving parent will often select the second alternative when designating a friend or child as attorney-in-fact in order to delegate authority only when necessary. The attorney-in-fact is accountable to the principal during the principal's lifetime and eventually to the deceased principal's personal representative after the principal is deceased.

Healthcare Power of Attorney/Declaration to Physicians (Living Will). Healthcare decisions can be made for you under a Healthcare Power of Attorney. A **healthcare agent** can be given the authority to make virtually all medical decisions on your behalf if you wish to have him or her do so. A number of medical decisions cannot be made by the healthcare agent, including long-term placement in a mental health facility and withholding of oral nutrition and hydration, without prior written consent. A number of other authorities can be given to or can be withheld from the healthcare agent, as specified under the Healthcare Power of Attorney form.

Old Talk New Conversations

In addition to or as part of a Healthcare Power of Attorney, you can have a Declaration to Physicians (also known as a **Living Will**). The Declaration to Physicians is a limited direction that requires your physicians to terminate life-support systems and tube feeding, if so desired, in the event of your terminal illness or brain death. A Declaration to Physicians can be signed separately from a Healthcare Power of Attorney form or can be incorporated into the terms of a Healthcare Power of Attorney form.

Joint Ownership. You can hold some or all of your assets in joint ownership with one or more persons. Under many joint ownership arrangements, such as for bank accounts, either joint owner has the authority to manage the assets. Under other joint ownership arrangements, as for real estate and securities, all joint owners must act together. A potential risk with joint ownership of assets is the effect of a joint ownership at death; that is, upon your death, the other joint owner(s) will own the asset completely and will not be required to share the asset(s) with any other of your beneficiaries.

Example #1: Jane

Jane, a widow, had three children, two of whom lived in other parts of the country and one of whom, Mary, lived in the same city. Jane put all of her accounts into joint names with Mary to allow Mary to handle Jane's banking and investments. After Jane's death, Mary had to pay gift tax when she divided the joint accounts, with her siblings. Jane avoided probate on the joint accounts but created a gift tax for Mary.

ESTATE AND TAX PLANNING

Example #2: Robert

Robert, a widower, had four children, and named his son, John, as joint owner of all of Robert's accounts. After Robert's death, John's creditors seized all of John's assets, including the funds received from his father. None of Robert's other children received any part of their inheritance.

Living Trust. You can create a Living Trust (which will be discussed in greater detail below) and transfer some or all of your assets to the Living Trust during your lifetime. In the event of your disability assets in the trust will be managed by a successor trustee. The successor trustee can then manage your business and financial affairs in the event of your disability. An additional benefit of a Living Trust is that assets in the Living Trust avoid probate in your estate after your death. Later in this chapter we will discuss probate and why you may choose to avoid probate for your heirs.

Other. Finally, in limited circumstances other legal entities can be used to provide financial management in the event of your disability. For example, partnerships, corporations, and limited liability companies can, in relatively rare circumstances, be used as property management vehicles for a disabled person.

Transfers after Death

After your death your assets must be transferred to your intended beneficiaries. There are two basic types of asset transfers after death, probate and nonprobate. Within nonprobate transfers there are a multitude of methods that avoid probate.

Old Talk *New Conversations*

Probate. The term "probate" simply refers to the court-supervised process of transferring a deceased person's assets and clearing that deceased person's debts. Probate and taxes are not the same, and probate does not define which of your beneficiaries receive your assets. Probate simply means that the local court has a role in overseeing the transfer of your assets after your death.

Assets that are subject to probate are distributed according to the terms of your will, if you have one; if you do not have a will, then they are distributed pursuant to the laws of intestacy (dying without a valid will). The laws of intestacy require that probate assets that are not effectively disposed of by the will must pass to the heirs-at-law of the deceased person. The heirs-at-law basically include the surviving spouse, if any, and sometimes children, grandchildren, and other lineal descendants. If you are not survived by a spouse or lineal descendants, then other blood relatives are the "heirs."

If you have a will, then probate assets will pass under the terms of the will. The will can leave the assets directly to one or more beneficiaries or to a trust, or the will itself can create a trust for one or more of your beneficiaries. If the trust is created under your will, it is called a **testamentary trust**, and its operations will be subject to the court's supervision.

Many people today want to avoid probate. In some parts of the country "probate avoidance" is almost an industry in itself. Probate is generally more time-consuming, more public, and more bureaucratic than nonprobate transfers. Also, in some locations the costs involved in probate can be higher, perhaps significantly higher, than if probate is avoided.

On the other hand, probate serves several very important uses, such as:

- Clearing all debts of the decedent (deceased person),
- Clearing ownership of the decedent's assets, and
- Clearing all claims by or against a decedent and the decedent's estate.

For relatively modest estates the costs of probating the estate can be equal to or less than the costs of avoiding probate. In these situations probate must be *completely* avoided for all of the estate. Having "a little bit" of probate is like being "a little bit" pregnant; even a little bit of probate involves time, energy, and costs.

Nonprobate. There are many more forms of nonprobate transfers than there are of probate transfers. The most typical nonprobate transfers are **living trusts, joint ownership, life estate deeds, beneficiary designation, Washington Will** (for married couples only), and **payable on death (POD)** or **transfer on death (TOD)** accounts. Assets that pass without probate are generally not governed by a will, and so it is important to coordinate the intended beneficiaries of both probate and nonprobate transfers.

Living Trust—A living trust can be either revocable or irrevocable. Many people use revocable living trusts in their estate planning in order to allow them to update the terms of their estate planning. Living trusts can also include tax planning provisions, which will be discussed later in this chapter. The terms of the living trust can be used to make outright gifts to your beneficiaries, or to continue trusts for the beneficiaries.

Old Talk *New Conversations*

A living trust can also be irrevocable, and people who create irrevocable trusts do so as part of their tax planning. The many tax planning uses of irrevocable trusts are too complicated for us to address in this book. If you want more information about using irrevocable trusts in your planning, consult a knowledgeable, competent attorney.

Joint Ownership—Another form of nonprobate transfer is joint ownership. Under a joint ownership each of the joint owners owns an equal portion of the asset, and the asset passes directly to the surviving owner(s) after death. The surviving owner(s) is not required to share the joint asset with any of your other beneficiaries.

For married persons joint ownership (or survivorship marital property, tenancy by the entireties, or other similar concepts) works very well to avoid probate of the first spouse's estate. However, after the first spouse's death, the surviving spouse must then take action to avoid probate on these assets. So for married couples joint ownership is a probate deferral, rather than a probate avoidance, technique.

Life Estate Deed—A life estate deed typically relates to a specified piece of real estate. The owner of the property (called the **life tenant**) typically deeds the property to someone else (called the **remainderman**) and reserves the right to use and occupy—or receive the rental income from—the property for the rest of the life tenant's life. Upon the death of the life tenant the property passes without probate to the remainderman.

A serious drawback to using life estate deeds is the inflexibility that the arrangement creates. That is, the remainderman must join in most decisions affecting the property. Also, if the life tenant wishes to change the remainderman, the remainderman must give his or her consent, and there may be tax consequences of the change of ownership. Finally, if the remainderman predeceases the life tenant, then the remainderman's interest in the property is subject to probate in the remainderman's estate.

Beneficiary Designations—Beneficiary designations apply for many types of assets. The most typical assets that use beneficiary designations are life insurance policies, annuities, IRAs, and other retirement benefits. After the owner's death the proceeds are paid directly from the insurance company under the life insurance policy or annuity contract, from the IRA custodian, or from the retirement plan trustee. Under a beneficiary designation form you can divide the asset among one or more beneficiaries, you can pay the benefit out directly to those beneficiaries, you can pay the asset into a trust, and, in some cases, you can define how the benefit will be payable to your beneficiaries. A beneficiary designation can almost always be changed as desired by the asset owner.

Payable on Death (POD) Accounts/Transfer on Death (TOD) Securities— Another form of nonprobate transfer is a POD account or a TOD security. These assets are owned completely by the person who is shown as the owner; at that person's death they are payable or transferable directly to the designated recipient or recipients. (The designated recipient can be one person or several people.) The payment of the account or transfer of the security can be directly to the beneficiary or it can be through a trust for that beneficiary. The POD account or TOD security can be sold, and the POD or TOD designation changed, without the consent of the designated beneficiary.

Marital Property Agreement—For married couples in Wisconsin a Washington Will provision of a Marital Property Agreement can be used to avoid probate. The Washington Will clause of the Marital Property Agreement specifies which asset or assets will pass after death to one or more beneficiaries. The Marital Property Agreement can specify that the transfers will occur only at the death of the husband or of the wife, or at the death of either the husband or the wife, or at the death of only the surviving spouse. The provisions of a Marital Property Agreement can often be modified or revoked by the surviving spouse even after the first spouse's death. If the couple does not want the surviving spouse to be able to amend the Washington Will clause, then the Marital Property Agreement can create a trust and hold assets in trust under the Marital Property Agreement.

People who wish to avoid probate often use one or more different techniques to assure that they accomplish their goal. For example, a person may transfer some properties to his or her Living Revocable Trust and then designate life insurance or IRAs to be payable to beneficiaries under beneficiary designations. Married couples may also use a Washington Will Marital Property Agreement to pick up any assets that were not transferred by other methods in order to better assure that all assets pass to the designated beneficiaries without probate.

Even when people use all of the probate avoidance techniques, they often will also use a **Pourover Will** to coordinate all

ESTATE AND TAX PLANNING

of their assets and, in some cases, to make tax elections. A Pourover Will leaves assets that are subject to probate to the Revocable Trust, and so "pour" the remaining assets into the Trust after death.

Tax Planning

Earlier in this chapter we discussed the importance of transferring property as part of your estate planning. The next part of this chapter reviews the income tax, gift tax, and estate tax consequences of transferring your property. You should consult with a competent legal advisor prior to implementing any estate plan.

Income Tax

Generally inheritances are received by the recipient free of income tax. A number of important exceptions apply. For example, income received by the heir and that was generated by the asset after the decedent's date of death will be subject to income tax. Likewise, certain types of assets (known as "income in respect of a decedent") will be subject to income tax even after the decedent's death. For example, deferred income, the unreported gain from installment sales, U.S. Savings Bond interest, IRAs, and interest and dividends accrued prior to death but paid after death are all income in the hands of the recipient.

The second significant income tax implication relates to capital gains taxes. Generally speaking, for capital gains tax purposes an heir receives a new cost basis in assets received from a decedent. The new basis equals the value of the assets in the decedent's estate. This basis adjustment is typically referred to as a "basis step-up" at death, although if the value of an asset is

Old Talk New Conversations

lower than the basis in the hands of the decedent immediately before death, then a basis "step-down" occurs at death. The result of the basis adjustment at death is to eliminate the capital gain or capital loss that the decedent would have had on a taxable disposition of assets immediately before death. For married couples in marital property and community property states, the basis adjustment applies to both the husband's and the wife's halves of marital property and community property upon the death of either spouse, provided that the deceased spouse's interest in the asset was subject to estate tax in that spouse's estate.

Gift Tax

The gift tax applies to gifts that you make during your life. Most gifts between married couples are exempt from the gift tax. In addition, the first $10,000 of **present interest** gifts per donor per donee each year are exempt from the gift tax. Likewise, tuition payments that are made directly to an educational organization and medical care payments that are made directly to the provider are exempt from gift tax.

Gifts that do not qualify for the marital deduction, the annual exclusion, or the medical and educational expense exclusion must be reported for gift tax purposes and will create a gift tax consequence. However, no gift tax will be payable until the donor's **applicable exclusion amount** has been fully used. The applicable exclusion amount in 1999 is $650,000 and is scheduled to increase according to the following table:

CHART 1
APPLICABLE EXCLUSION AMOUNT

Gifts Made, or Deaths Occurring, On or After January 1	Applicable Exclusion Amount
1999	$ 650,000
2000	675,000
2002	700,000
2004	850,000
2005	950,000
2006	$ 1,000,000

Estate Tax

The estate tax applies to the value of a decedent's estate. Most assets that are owned by the decedent or that are controlled by the decedent are subject to estate tax. This ranges from assets owned directly by the decedent, to assets held in a revocable trust for the decedent, to life insurance on the decedent's life, to the decedent's interest in joint assets, and even to assets that the decedent has transferred during his or her lifetime if the decedent retained an income from or control over those assets. In some limited cases the estate tax can also apply to assets that were transferred within three years of the decedent's death.

The estate tax allows a deduction for gifts to charity. Likewise, the estate tax allows a deduction for most transfers to the decedent's surviving spouse.

Old Talk New Conversations

The estate tax allows an exemption on an amount equal to the "applicable exclusion amount." The applicable exclusion amounts are shown in Chart 1.

The value of a decedent's taxable estate in excess of the charitable deduction, the marital deduction, the qualified family-owned business interest deduction, and other exclusions and deductions is subject to estate tax. The following chart shows the estate tax brackets.

CHART 2
ESTATE TAX BRACKETS

Taxable Estate At Least	But Not More Than	Federal Estate Tax Bracket (Includes State Death Tax Credit)
$ 650,000	$ 750,000	37%
750,000	1,000,000	39
1,250,000	1,000,000	41
1,250,000	1,500,000	43
1,500,000	2,000,000	45
2,000,000	2,500,000	49
2,500,000	3,000,000	53
3,000,000	10,000,000	55
10,000,000	21,040,000	60
$21,040,000	—	55

A married couple's typical estate plan sets up a trust at the first spouse's death that will support the surviving spouse for the rest of that surviving spouse's lifetime and eventually pass tax-free to the couple's children. Any excess of the deceased spouse's assets above the "applicable exclusion amount" (and other deductions or exclusions) is left directly to the surviving spouse or to a qualifying marital deduction trust.

The most typical type of marital deduction trust is a **qualified terminable interest property (QTIP)** trust. For married couples in Wisconsin another typical type of marital deduction trust is a **power of withdrawal** or **power of appointment** marital trust. In a power of withdrawal trust the surviving spouse receives all of the trust's income for his or her entire life, and can withdraw as much or all of the trust as he or she wishes at any time. In a power of appointment marital trust the surviving spouse receives all of the trust's income for his or her entire life, and can leave the trust to whomever he or she wishes after his or her death.

The following two charts show typical estate plans for married couples. Chart 3 shows the estate plan where a joint trust is utilized by the married couple. Chart 4 shows the estate plan where each spouse has separate wills and revocable trusts.

Where the estate tax liability to be paid by the children is sufficiently large, the person may choose to create liquidity at his or her death to pay the estate tax. Often this liquidity is created by life insurance, and the insurance is typically owned by someone other than the insured person. Often an irrevocable trust that is designed to own the policy is created and then acquires the insurance policy. In this way the insurance proceeds are available to the family to assist with the payment of the estate tax, although the insurance proceeds are not, themselves, subject to estate tax.

OldTalk *New Conversations*

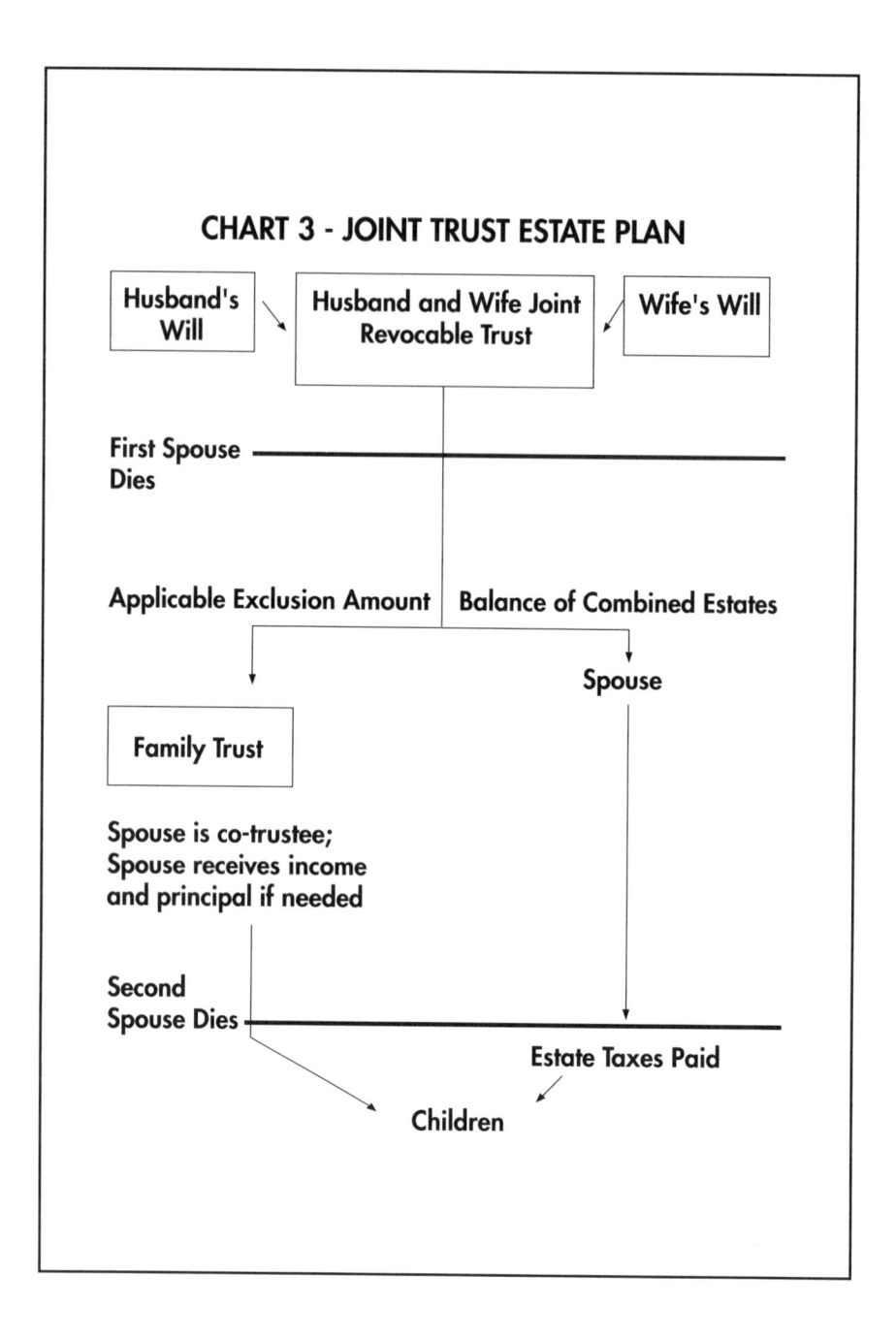

CHART 3 - JOINT TRUST ESTATE PLAN

[Husband's Will] → [Husband and Wife Joint Revocable Trust] ← [Wife's Will]

First Spouse Dies

- Applicable Exclusion Amount → **Family Trust**
  - Spouse is co-trustee; Spouse receives income and principal if needed
- Balance of Combined Estates → **Spouse**

Second Spouse Dies

→ Children
→ Estate Taxes Paid

ESTATE AND TAX PLANNING

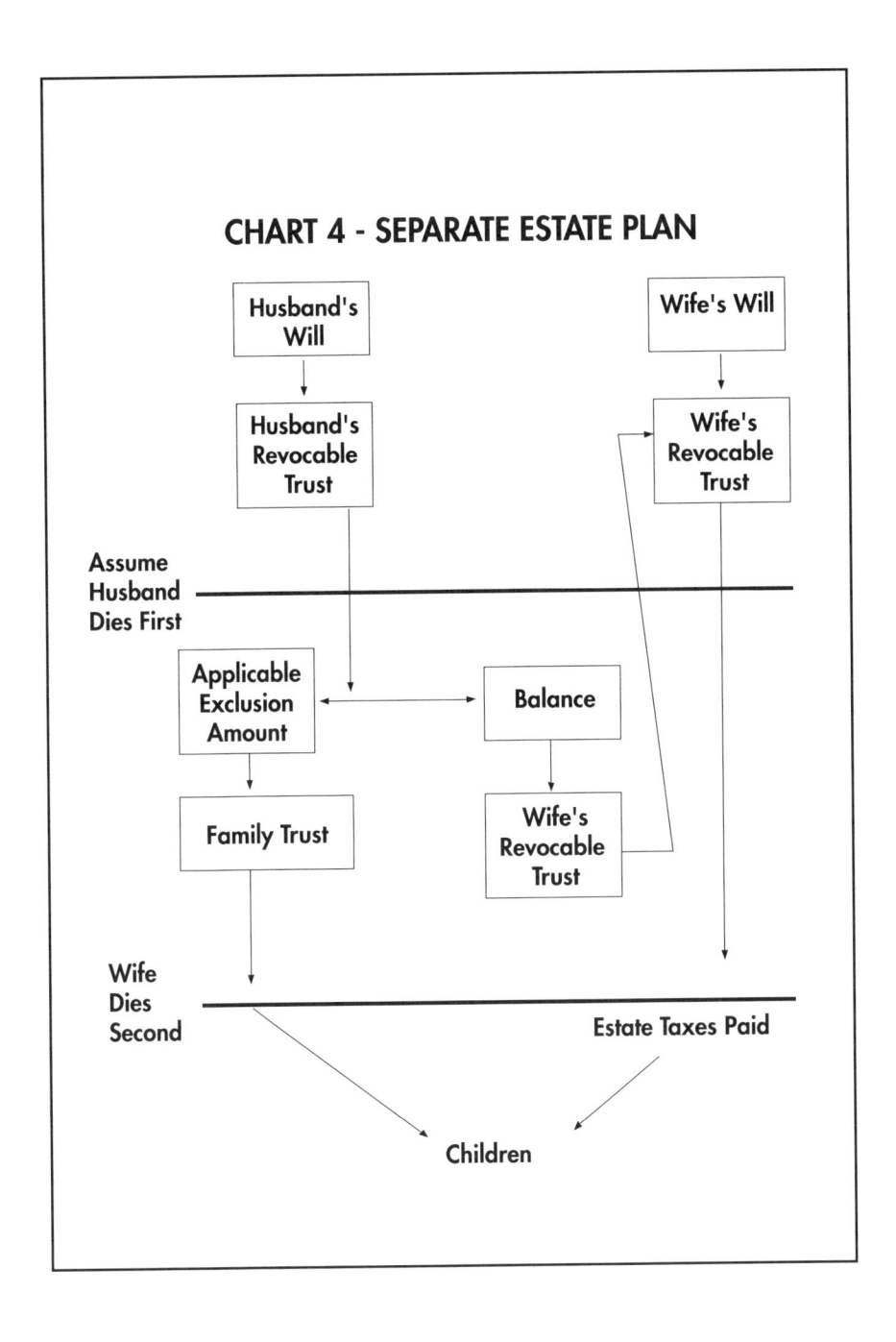

CHART 4 - SEPARATE ESTATE PLAN

```
    Husband's Will                        Wife's Will
         ↓                                    ↓
    Husband's                             Wife's
    Revocable                             Revocable
    Trust                                 Trust
         |
─────────|──────────────────────────────────────────
Assume   |
Husband  |
Dies First
         ↓
    Applicable
    Exclusion  ←→   Balance
    Amount              ↓
         ↓          Wife's
    Family Trust    Revocable
                    Trust
         |
─────────|──────────────────────────────────────────
Wife                          Estate Taxes Paid
Dies
Second          ↘         ↙
                 Children
```

CHAPTER THREE

◆

LONG-TERM CARE INSURANCE—
THE NEW FINANCIAL NECESSITY

BY STEVEN J. KOPPEL, CLU, ChFC

Long-term care insurance is the new financial necessity, because retirement is now so often followed by an extended period of disability. In this chapter we will explore the changes in health, demographics, and finances that have led to the creation of long-term care insurance, plus discuss the structure of long-term care insurance, how to buy it, and from whom.

The New Generation Gap

The "Generation Gap" of the 1960s and 1970s was about alienation, misunderstanding, and rebellions of youth. The new generation gap is about living long past retirement, something that only rarely occurred in the past.

In the year 200 BC life expectancy was about 22 years. In the year 1900 life expectancy was 45 years. In other words, before this century it took several generations before the life expectancy of the average person would increase even a year. Today the average life expectancy is 75 years. In less than 100 years life expectancy

OldTalk New Conversations

has almost doubled. The generation now beginning to retire feels anxious as they face new financial decisions because they are likely to have 20 to 40 more years of life. This anxiety comes because there is nothing in their past family histories or generational experience (i.e., there is a "gap") to give them a road map for planning today's long-life-expectancy issues.

Not only are people living longer, but they are also enjoying better health. Medical technology, changing dietary habits, and the reduction of tobacco use has made today's older Americans the strongest and healthiest of all time. However, no one lasts forever, and eventually we all succumb to a final aging process. Few people today live into their late 80s and beyond without needing some form of assistance. Few people presently in advanced old age thought they would ever live that long, and they often did not do financial planning expecting to live so long a life. Long-term care insurance was developed to help pay the cost of this final period of life when care is most likely to be needed.

The Numbers: Who Will Use Long-Term Care Insurance?

Living in the United States today an individual over age 65 has a 70 percent chance of needing some form of assisted caregiving. Of those, 40 percent will end up in a nursing home, involving a stay of at least 90 days. These are the statistics for a single person. It becomes obvious that when considering a couple, both over age 65, the statistical probability of at least one of them living into his or her late 80s or 90s and requiring some type of caregiving assistance is high. Thus, making decisions as to the type of care and making choices as to where and how one will live out the final part of life becomes a critical part of financial planning.

The Role of Government in Elder Care

In the 1970s and 1980s it was common practice to divest assets in order to qualify for government benefits (that is, Medicaid) that would pay for nursing home care. That strategy is becoming more difficult for two reasons. First, government as a whole is shrinking. As the American public wants less and not more government, government's role as a provider of welfare benefits is increasingly being reduced, with the result being fewer dollars available for these programs.

The second important factor is the rapidly expanding aging population. The chart on the following page illustrates the aging of America. In the year 2035, when the baby boomers will be in their 80s and 90s, that percentage of the elderly population will be fifty percent larger than it is today. Thus, today there are more elderly people trying to use a shrinking pool of dollars, putting enormous strain on the system.

Because of these government and demographic changes, public assistance in the form of Medicaid will remain a benefit only for the most indigent.

Caregivers Now and Then

Caregiving options have also changed dramatically in the last generation. If we were to look back to the middle of the 20th century, we would see primarily one-income families still clustered in their cities of origin and multigenerational family members living in close proximity to one another. As children would leave the home, their mother would have the time to care for her aging parents or in-laws because her childrearing responsibilities were over and she often did not work outside of the home.

OldTalk New Conversations

CHART 1
PROJECTED DISTRIBUTION OF THE ELDERLY POPULATION BY AGE (1985 – 2050)*

Percent of Elderly Population

Age Group	1985	2010	2035	2050
65-69	32.2	29.9	24.0	24.6
70-74	26.6	21.8	24.3	20.0
75-79	19.6	17.4	21.0	17.1
80-84	12.2	14.0	14.8	14.5
85 & over	9.4	16.9	16.0	23.7
Total	100.0	100.0	100.0	100.0

*Total may not add to 100 because of rounding.
Source: Computed from Bureau of Census, Publication Series P-25, No. 952, 1984.

The structure of the American family has fundamentally changed in the last 50 years. Two-income families are the rule rather than the exception. Some married couples are postponing having children into their 30s and 40s. This means that as parents age, their children do not have the time or financial resources to provide care.

In addition to changing family dynamics, the new wealth of older Americans gives them greater lifestyle choices than ever before. The last 25 years of the 20th century saw an unprecedented growth in equity investments around the world. Millionaires have been created routinely by the vast wealth that has become concentrated in individual stock portfolios. Many maintain two homes and may live a significant part of the time away from their children, who are also on the move. New economic centers have been created in the last part of the 20th century, moving children into new locales where there is greater economic opportunity. The result of these changes is that when an older individual finally needs the services of a caregiver, there may not be a family member available to help, as had often been the case in prior generations.

A new set of caregiving alternatives has appeared. These alternatives recognize that elderly persons may go through a series of living arrangements in the last part of their lives based on their caregiving needs. Each transition will require a little more assistance than the last but will also involve maintaining as much independence as possible. Where nursing homes were the only option as recently as 25 years ago, assisted living facilities, community-based residential facilities, and home healthcare allow individuals to remain in their own homes or move into a facility with supplemental services while still maintaining their own household.

Who Pays for Care?

To understand who pays for care, it is important to distinguish between acute versus chronic illness. An **acute illness** or injury is a health problem that develops unexpectedly and is one from which the individual may recover. The key concept here is that the person will get better. The costs of caring for an acutely ill person are typically covered with health insurance or by Medicare. With an acute illness the individual's care starts at a hospital, and recovery is usually completed at home. Examples of this type of health problem are broken bones, heart attack, or stroke.

A **chronic illness** is an illness or injury that the individual will not recover from although his or her functioning may improve. It is usually progressive in nature, meaning that it gets worse over time. Examples of this type of health problem are arthritis, Parkinson's Disease, and Alzheimer's Disease. The cost of care for a chronic illness is always paid by the individual; however, a great deal of the care can be provided by family and friends at no cost.

Who Should Buy Long-Term Care Insurance?

I believe that everyone should consider having long-term care insurance regardless of his or her financial circumstances. Let's look at three real-life examples from very different financial circumstances to understand the need for long-term care insurance.

Example # 1: Fred and Ethel

Fred and Ethel have been married for 50 years and are 76 and 74 years of age, respectively. Their home is fully paid for, and they have liquid assets of $400,000. They have five children, two of whom are in their late 40s and have not been financially successful. Ethel has had an ongoing battle with dementia that has recently escalated to the point where Fred can no longer take care of her at home; sadly, he is going to place her in a care facility that specializes in dementia. He is concerned about preserving his estate for two reasons. First, he would like to reserve some money for his own caregiver needs, but more importantly, he feels a strong need to make sure that there is money in his estate for his two children who have not been successful.

LONG-TERM CARE INSURANCE—THE NEW FINANCIAL NECESSITY

Fred and Ethel face a significant problem because they are going to be maintaining two households on an income that had previously been used for only one. The cost of care for Ethel will be paid by Fred because their assets are too large to qualify for Medicaid benefits. Fred runs a significant risk of depleting their assets to care for Ethel, with the result being fewer dollars available for care if Fred should need it and fewer dollars available to pass on to his children. It should be noted that specialized care facilities, such as those for dementia and Alzheimer's Disease, are typically more expensive than non-specialized facilities.

Long-term care is appropriate in this situation as an asset protection tool. It assures Fred that there will be funds available for his care, and the insurance will conserve assets so that there may be funds available to his children at his death.

Unfortunately, at this point Ethel is uninsurable. An existing cognitive impairment is typically a cause for being denied long-term care insurance. Good health is always a special commodity when insurance is desired. Everyone ultimately loses insurability; hopefully that happens after all of the insurance that is needed has been purchased. Because of the financial squeeze that Fred faces, his children may want to help pay the long-term care policy premiums.

Example #2: Rob and Laura

Rob and Laura are in their mid-70s. They have a mixed portfolio of stocks and bonds worth one million dollars, plus Rob has a pension plan. Between their income from Social Security, the pension plan, and minimum distributions from their IRAs, they

OldTalk *New Conversations*

have a very comfortable life and want for nothing. In fact, their portfolio continues to grow. They live in Florida and have three sons who are scattered all over the country.

Unfortunately, a million dollars is not what it used to be. The risk here is similar to the one facing Fred and Ethel. That is, if one spouse needs significant care expenses, it could eat into the asset portfolio that would be available to the surviving healthy spouse. Additionally, if Rob were to die first, Laura will likely see a reduction in pension income, which in turn may cause her to spend down her estate principal. Since their asset base is continuing to grow, it would be very easy for them to afford the premium by merely diverting some of the interest or dividends earned on their investments to premium payments. This would not impact their lifestyle at all and give them great peace of mind.

Additionally, the tax benefits available in a tax-qualified, long-term care insurance plan make this an excellent asset-management tool. If they are forced to use principal to pay for caregiving costs, they will incur either ordinary income tax or capital gains tax in liquidating parts of their portfolio. Benefits received from long-term care insurance are income tax free, plus the premiums paid for a tax-qualified, long-term care insurance plan are included in the definition of "medical expenses" and thus may be eligible for an income tax deduction, subject to certain limitations.

Example # 3: Rhoda

Rhoda is a 65-year-old widow. Her husband ran a successful business, which is now professionally managed and has a market value of approximately four million dollars. As Chairman *of the Board, she is paid an income of $250,000 a year. Additionally she has an IRA that is worth one million dollars. She has four children who get along but have very different lifestyles and economic situations. A few years earlier her mother died after an extended period of caregiving that was at first provided in her home and eventually transitioned into a skilled nursing facility. Rhoda and her brother disagreed over the type of care that was provided for her mother, which led to a strained relationship between the two. She wants to avoid this in her family.*

All too often we focus on the financial reasons for buying long-term care insurance. However, it is equally important to look at the nonfinancial reasons. Having a disabled and dependent parent is one of the most difficult things for children to deal with. Many people who have gone through this process have little advance warning or guidance as to how to make decisions for their parents, particularly when they have had no prior conversations with their parents about their wishes. Further complicating the problem is that, potentially for the first time in the parent/child relationship, the child must act for the parent in a parent-like role. This is a difficult transition to make under any circumstances, but to do it in a period of ill health or emergency becomes extraordinarily stressful. A long-term care policy can diffuse some of the stressful decisions that need to be made for sick and elderly parents who can no longer make decisions for themselves.

One of the great psychological benefits of owning any form of insurance is peace of mind. For example, Rhoda owns fire insurance on her home, which is currently valued at $500,000. Clearly she has the financial resources to rebuild her home in the event of a fire without having to purchase insurance. However she chooses to insure the risk because it gives her peace of mind, and she would rather not pay this cost from her existing assets. I find that many wealthier clients have the same reaction to caregiving costs. This is something they simply do not want to pay out of their assets. One of the great concerns of all older people, no matter what their financial circumstances, is the fear of outliving their assets. Long-term care insurance can go a long way toward easing those concerns because that is usually the greatest financial risk people face in the last part of their lives.

Recent legislation has provided numerous tax benefits for long-term care insurance. A business entity can buy long-term care insurance for any employee and deduct the premium. A deduction can equal the entire cost of the premium or part of it, depending on the type of entity and age of the employee. In this case the entire premium could be deducted in her business.

Long-Term Care Insurance Is about Choices

The decision to buy long-term care insurance is really a decision about choice. It is a decision about ending your days in dignity and in the manner *you*, not your children, choose. Without insurance benefits children and personal representatives have to make difficult decisions about how and when to liquidate assets and what level of care to provide for the individual needing help. Conflicts can arise between siblings or other family members over these issues, which can have a damaging effect on family relationships. By creating a pool of money specifically allocated to caregiving costs, the decision-making process around these issues is made much easier for everyone concerned and gives certainty to the insureds that they will end their days comfortably and in a way that they have chosen.

The Structure and Taxation of a Long-Term Care Policy

Tax Status of Benefits. Buying long-term care insurance has become greatly simplified with passage of the Health Insurance Portability and Accountability Act of 1996 (also known as the Kennedy-Kassenbaum Bill), which clarified the tax status of long-term care insurance. It created a structure for long-term care policies to follow in order for benefits to be received free of income tax. A policy that follows these federal guidelines is known as a "qualified" long-term care policy and has all of the tax benefits that are provided under law. **Tax-qualified policies** represent the majority of policies being sold in the marketplace today. It is possible to buy non-tax-qualified policies; however, this chapter will discuss only tax-qualified policies.

Receiving Benefits from a Long-Term Care Policy. Long-term care insurance is one of the simplest types of policies sold by the insurance industry. Typically for an insured person to receive benefits, a licensed healthcare practitioner will have certified in the last 12 months that the potential insured person has needed hands-on or standby assistance to perform at least two of the six **activities of daily living (ADL)** for at least 90 days due to a loss of functional capacity, or has required substantial supervision to protect him or herself from threats to health and safety due to a severe cognitive impairment. The six activities of daily living are:

bathing, transferring, dressing, continence, toileting, and eating.

Additionally, the insurance company needs to determine that these expenses are being received for qualified long-term care services from appropriate providers of care, such as nursing homes, alternative living facilities, adult day-care facilities, or home healthcare agencies.

Most of the policies today will pay the benefits whether services are provided in a care facility or at home. The packaging of home healthcare with facility care varies from company to company, so close attention needs to be paid to the structure of the contract. Since statistics show that over 80 percent of care today is provided in the home, it is strongly advised that you look for a policy that will pay whether the services are delivered at home or in a care facility.

Pricing a Long-Term Care Policy. Three important variables will determine the premium of a long-term care policy. The first relates to the amount of benefits you want to have. Most policies express these benefits in the form of a per-day rate, which is how nursing homes and home healthcare providers charge for their services. You need to be aware of what the costs of services are in your area. I am writing this chapter in the Midwest, where the average per-day rate for basic care in a nursing home hovers between $140 to $165 per day. The services of a licensed home healthcare aide typically run approximately $15 per hour. In certain parts of the country these costs may be slightly lower, but in other parts of the country these rates can be almost double.

The second major cost variable is the date upon which benefits begin. The most common starting date is either 91 or 181 days after an individual first requires service. If an individual has a hospital stay prior to his or her use of a care facility, Medicare may provide benefits for the first 90 days of care. Note that there are policies that offer earlier starting dates, which will raise the premiums, and there are options that offer later starting dates, which will reduce premiums.

The third variable of premium cost is how long you wish to receive benefits. Typical benefit periods are lifetime, six years, four years, or three years. The longer the benefit period is, the higher the premium.

Let's look at an example. Assume a 70-year-old male purchases a policy with a 91-day wait, benefits of $100 per day, and a six-year benefit period. This means that the policy will begin to pay 91 days after he first requires services based on the need for hands-on assistance with at least two of the six ADLs or needing substantial supervision to maintain his health and safety due to a cognitive impairment. He will be reimbursed up to $100 a day for the costs he incurs. This works out to $35,600 a year or, over a six-year period, $219,000. Most insurance companies look at these benefits in the aggregate and call this a "pool of money." If total benefits are not used up in a given year, they will carry over into future years and be available to the insured if he or she has continued expenses. In our example if the insured were to incur costs of only $50 a day, he would only be using half of his total benefits in any given year. Therefore, if his costs never exceed $50 a day, his benefits would actually last 12 years instead of 6 because that is how long it would take the insurance company to pay out $219,000 to him.

It should always be remembered that pricing not only

Old Talk New Conversations

depends on the decisions made in selecting these three variables, but also on one's age. The younger someone is, the less expensive it is to acquire a policy. **Most people should start to look at long-term care insurance after the age of 50, since prior to that time most dollars should be focused on retirement savings and developing net worth.**

Optional Benefits. Two optional benefits predominate in the industry. These benefits add to the overall premium of a policy and enhance the value of the policy but are not critical to its basic structure.

The first and most important optional benefit is indexing the policy for inflation. For most purchasers it will be 10, 20, or 30 years before benefits are finally received. During that time inflation will eat away at the purchasing power of the policy. It is critical that a policy has some form of inflation adjustment so that its buying power is maintained. This is done in two ways. The first is to pay a larger up-front premium to include this benefit but not have premiums increase annually. This is an **Automatic Benefit Increase**, but the actual names for the benefit can vary from company to company. Often there will be a choice as to the rate of inflation that may be applied to the policy.

The second form of indexing is an **Automatic Additional Purchase Benefit**. The premium for a policy with this benefit starts out much lower but goes up each year based on a rate of inflation. This particular option tends to be governed by state law, with 5 percent used as the inflation rate in most jurisdictions.

The other major optional benefit is called the **Paid-Up-Non-Forfeiture Benefit**. This benefit allows an individual to stop paying premiums after a certain amount of time and to use the accumulated premiums paid or 30 times the nursing home maximum daily limit, whichever is greater, to remain available as a permanent, long-term care benefit.

There may be other types of optional benefits available in the marketplace, so this list is not meant to be all inclusive. The operation of these benefits may also vary by state according to applicable state law.

Choosing an Insurance Company

An insurance contract is a contract of faith. You pay a premium with the expectation of receiving value. However, that value is only promised, not guaranteed. An insurance policy will only perform as well as the insurance company it is written from; therefore, it is important to buy your insurance from the best possible insurance company.

The financial strength of the insurance company is a critical factor in measuring the quality of an insurance company, because the performance of this contract will be years into the future, and you want to have the peace of mind that this particular insurance company is likely to be around when those benefits are paid. Not only is it important for that carrier to be around, it should be there in the same form and structure that it was when you originally purchased the policy.

The insurance industry is in a period of great change. Companies are merging, they are changing their operating structures, and some are even disposing of their field force. When a company is bought, merges, reorganizes, or merely has bad claim experience, the policyholders may be treated differently from what they expected or were told originally. An example would be premiums being raised. One of the biggest, if not the biggest, concerns in the Long Term Care industry is that current pricing is being set too low. We have already seen a number of price increases, some rather significant, on older policies. In several states this has led to law suits and proposed legislation that would protect consumers. A premium increase is particularly burdensome for older people who are on fixed incomes and have limited resources to assume higher premiums. By selecting a strong company up front, you have a better chance of avoiding uncertainty later.

Very few patients in nursing homes are currently receiving benefits under long-term care policies, since the majority of contracts have not been around long enough to mature into benefits. This means that the claims-paying ability of many companies has not been tested nearly as much as it will be in the coming years.

The good news about financial strength is that the information you need to compare companies to one another is readily available and easy to use. The industry uses four major rating services to monitor the financial strength of any given company. The chart on page 64 shows the rating services and their ranking categories.

The rankings these rating services produce is public information and can be retrieved at your local library, over the Internet, or by contacting the companies directly. You should be able to get this information from an agent as part of the fact finding you do in purchasing a policy. The key to remember in using these services is that the higher rating is better. Most of the major companies are rated by all four of the rating services. As a general rule, I recommend that a company should have at least one top rating from one of these rating services in order to be considered as a carrier to use for the purchase of long-term care policy.

Contractual Provisions

Most of the policies sold today are tax-qualified policies, and their basic contractual provisions are very similar. Companies will use different language to say essentially the same thing; therefore, comparing contract language can be a difficult exercise that can easily confuse you and overshadow the importance of other factors like company financial strength or the expertise and services of the agent. Additionally, many companies have unusual contract features that an agent may emphasize in order to differentiate his or her policy from others. Consumer advocates feel that it is the quality of the company more than any contract language that will determine the performance of the policy in the future.

Insurance companies have a way to adjust their policies if their actual experience turns bad, which is by merely raising the premium. You can always promise something as long as you reserve the right to break that promise. Thus, if an insurance company finds itself sustaining losses on contracts that were inappropriately structured, it merely has to increase the premiums to meet its claims expenses. This is why it is important to pick companies with strong financial ratings, because the ratings are used within the industry as a measure of good quality.

OldTalk New Conversations

CHART 2
INDEPENDENT RATING SERVICES

FINANCIAL STRENGTH			CLAIMS PAYING ABILITY	
A.M. Best Company (900) 555-2378 www.ambest.com	**Moody's Investors Service** (212) 553-0377 www.moodys.com	**Standard & Poor's®** (212) 208-1527 www.standard and poors.com/ratings	**Duff & Phelps Credit Rating Co.** (312) 368-3157 www.dcrco.com
Superior A++ A+	Exceptional Aaa	Superior AAA, AAAq*	Highest AAA
Excellent A A-	Excellent Aa1 Aa2 Aa3	Excellent AA+ AA, AAq AA-	Very High AA+ AA AA-
Very Good B++ B+	Good A1 A2 A3	Good A+ A, Aq A-	High A+ A A-
Adequate/ Vulnerable B B-	Adequate Baa1 Baa2 Baa3	Adequate BBB+ BBB, BBBq BBB-	Adequate BBB+ BBB BBB-
Vulnerable C+ to F	Weak Ba1 to C	Vulnerable BB+ to R BBq to CCCq	Non-Investment Grade BB+ to CCC-

* A letter "q" designates ratings for companies that did not actually request ratings. These ratings are based on quantitative analysis only from public data.

Some services use category qualifiers to further subdivide their ratings into as many as 22 different levels.

This report is not meant to suggest the replacement of an existing policy, or for comparison of product lines other than long-term care.

Selecting an Insurance Agent

Unlike insurance companies, which have adopted standard measurement techniques by which to compare themselves, there is not a comparable qualitative process to use for an insurance agent. Nevertheless, there are some certifications and expertise to your look for and to be sensitive to in making your selection. By no means should you ever feel pressured by an agent to make any decisions. Purchasing a long-term care policy is one of the most important decisions you will make during the remainder of your life, and no undue pressure should be used to influence it.

Most helpful is to use the references of friends who have dealt with an agent and can verify their experience with a particular individual. An important certification to look for in an agent is whether he or she is a CLU. CLU stands for Chartered Life Underwriter and is a designation granted by the Society of Financial Professionals. In order to become a CLU, an individual will have passed a series of 10 national insurance exams. However, once those exams are passed, it would be important to know if the agent has continued his or her membership in the Society. Being an active member of the Society means that an agent is keeping up his or her knowledge and staying current with the industry. This is the best measure of qualitative agent performance that the industry has, because the Society has focused exclusively on knowledge and product information.

Another good measurement is whether an agent is a member of the Million Dollar Round Table. As a production-based honor, this designation will tell you that this agent is devoting a lot of time to the industry and not "dabbling" in the business.

Old Talk New Conversations

It is also relevant to ask what experience prospective agents have had working with senior citizens. Are they active in local estate-planning groups? Do they serve on any community boards that work with seniors? Unlike other industries that have well-defined specialty practices, the insurance industry does not identify specialty practices at this time, even though many agents do specialize in certain markets. It is incumbent on prospective buyers to ask as many questions as possible about the credentials and background of the agents with whom they are dealing.

CHAPTER FOUR

◆

GETTING THE CARE YOU NEED WHEN YOU LIVE AT HOME

BY PHYLLIS MENSH BROSTOFF, ACSW, CISW

All of the issues discussed in this book are complex and multifaceted. The decisions you make have implications for the future of your whole family, as well as for each individual member. After the children have grown up and moved out of the family home, family members often live relatively separate lives for many years, seeing each other primarily for special occasions, living lives quite independent of each other. Eventually, however, an event occurs, or a change happens, that stops the family in its tracks and demands a new approach. This can be a serious accident, an unexpected illness, a death, or the realization that slowly, over the course of many months or even years, a family member has ceased being completely competent.

When this happens, families can fall apart, or they can grow together. Old wounds, hurts, or misunderstandings can be reviewed and forgiven, allowing the family to reorganize itself to help a needy member. A new appreciation for the talents or expertise of each family member can allow everyone to see each

OldTalk New Conversations

other in a different way. Or stopgap, crisis-response measures can be used to handle the particular event, without addressing the possible changes needed in roles and responsibilities or in how decisions are made. This is the challenge—to have a new conversation on some rather difficult subjects when family members grow old.

Who Lives at Home?

Most people live and die in their own homes. Only 6.2 percent of all Wisconsin residents over age 65 live in a skilled nursing facility on any given day. In fact, in Wisconsin only 28 percent of people over the age of 85 live in a skilled nursing facility even though the rate nationally is 32 percent. Nursing home occupancy dropped significantly between 1980 and 1990, primarily because alternatives to nursing homes increased (see Chapter Five). A 1994 report by the Wisconsin Bureau on Aging found that 79 percent of people over 60 are homeowners, with 93 percent of them owning their homes outright. And most people over 60 live with a spouse, with only the oldest women (over 85) likely to be living alone. So if you are now married, you can reasonably expect to plan to continue to live in your own home, possibly with your spouse, for the rest of your life.

How Do People Make Decisions?

Families generally prefer to make decisions about care by themselves. However, for some families who are facing complex problems or need multiple services, a new professional specialty service known as **geriatric care management** has developed in the past decade. This service is provided by individuals trained as social workers, nurses, or geriatric counselors. The purpose of geriatric care management is to help families understand the issues and decisions they face, to identify options, and to recommend and arrange appropriate services and resources. You or your family can expect to pay a geriatric care manager's fee directly unless you have long-term care insurance, which may pay for it. Geriatric care managers usually charge by the hour, although some care managers charge flat fees.

A geriatric care manager can assist you and your family first by exploring the physical, emotional, financial, and social problems you are experiencing. This assessment includes understanding how you are functioning at home; the help you have available to you from family, friends, and neighbors; any medical conditions you are being treated for; and your financial situation. The geriatric care manager is then able to recommend ways to improve your functioning and provide you with information on the resources and service options available to you and the costs of these options.

After a plan is agreed upon, the care manager can arrange for the services you want and then continue to provide ongoing monitoring and reassessment as your condition changes over time. Geriatric care management can prove particularly useful for people who have no families, whose family members live far away, or who have changing circumstances or complex problems that have already proved to be difficult for the family to manage without professional advice.

Old Talk *New Conversations*

Example #1: Joan

Joan is an 83-year-old widow who has some loss of short-term memory, although her long-term memory is relatively good. Her only son lives in Washington State. Joan's physician questions whether she can continue to drive. He asked a geriatric care manager to see Joan because she had come to his office six times in two days trying to understand an invoice she received in the mail and to ask about a new medication he had prescribed. When the care manager met with Joan in her home, she could not find the phone number of her son, and the doctor did not have it. The care manager looked up the son's name and address on the Internet and sent him a short note explaining the circumstances through which she had met his mother, and her services and fees.

The son engaged the care manager to develop a plan for assisting his mother to remain at home, which he knew was her desire. The initial plan called for the care manager to visit Joan every two to three weeks, and to arrange for an aide to take her shopping and assist with housework three times a week. This assistance helped Joan agree to voluntarily give up driving. The care manager also purchased a medication box, which she filled during each visit. The care manager kept the son informed by mail or telephone concerning Joan's health status and social situation.

Licensed Home Health Services

If you are recovering from an acute illness, you may be eligible for **home health services** that are paid for by the Medicare program. If your doctor prescribes skilled nursing service, physical therapy, occupational therapy, or speech therapy *and* you are home-bound, Medicare will pay for these services.

In addition, you may also receive help from a home health aide, under the supervision of the professional nurse or therapist. Physical and occupational therapists can evaluate your home and recommend equipment (such as grab bars in the bathroom) that improves safety.

These services must be obtained from a licensed home health agency certified to provide Medicare-reimbursed services. These can be freestanding agencies, or they can be part of a large, hospital-based organization. These licensed home health services can last as long as the need for the skilled care continues, but once that need is met, all Medicare-reimbursable care ends.

Hospice Care

Hospice care is a special service that uses an interdisciplinary team approach to provide care and comfort to individuals and their families at the end of life. Hospice care is paid for by Medicare if a physician believes you have a life expectancy of six months or less. Although this service is currently used most frequently for people with cancer, it is available for any diagnosis as long as you agree that you want palliative, or comfort, measures, rather than medical attention that is expected to cure.

Realizing that one's life may be ending soon is, obviously, difficult to accept. It may be impossible for you to openly discuss your possible death with your family. Hospice's mission is to assist families in having a "good death." It is the philosophy of hospice services that the dying person should be pain free, in comfortable surroundings, cared for with dignity, and not alone. Many people speak generally about not wanting to be "kept alive by machines" but do not realize that even having an antibiotic for an infection is a form of treatment, since life saving antibiotics have become so commonplace.

While refusing treatment allows for the natural progression from life to death to occur, this is not a decision that you can make easily or quickly. Some people, even when their physician has made it very clear they are dying, continue to desire that all efforts be made to prolong life. You may wish to think about the philosophy of hospice services well before you may need them, and discuss your thoughts and feelings with your family.

Hospice care is provided by a specially trained team of physicians, nurses, aides, spiritual counselors, social workers, and volunteers, with on-call availability of professional staff to respond to any changes the family or other caregivers providing the 24-hour a day care notice in the person's medical condition. Hospice services also include any pain medication and equipment you may need. The hospice team's purpose is to assist the family throughout the dying process, so hospice service ends with bereavement counseling after death has occurred.

While most hospice care is provided to people in their own homes, hospice service is also available for respite care and inpatient care in nursing homes and special care units that are freestanding or affiliated with hospitals. These special inpatient hospice units often have no visiting hours, so families are free to come whenever they are able and to stay as long as they want. Some units have kitchens that families can use, comfortable recliners for family members, and other service components designed to help the whole family.

Unlicensed Home Care Services

Many other care services are provided in the home but are not licensed and not paid for by Medicare. One is an emergency response system, often called **Lifeline**, that allows people living alone to summon help even if they cannot get to the telephone. Lifeline is usually sponsored by a hospital or a licensed home health agency. Lifeline is installed on your home's telephone system (you need to have a touch-tone phone). Although there are several different designs of Lifeline systems, in the most typical system you carry a "button" on a chain that allows you to activate the Lifeline if you need to summon help. You will be asked to designate two or three "responders"—neighbors, friends, or family to whom you can give a key to your home—who will be contacted by Lifeline if you activate the emergency response system. When the responder comes into your home, he or she finds out why you called for help. If you need to go to the hospital, an ambulance is summoned. There is a one-time set-up fee and a modest monthly subscription cost to have Lifeline.

Meals on Wheels (also called **Mobile Meals**) provides one or two nutritional meals delivered daily to the home by volunteers at a very modest cost. The meals are delivered between 10:30 A.M. and 2:00 P.M., with a hot lunch for the midday meal and a sandwich, fruit, dessert, and milk or juice to be put in the refrigerator for the evening meal. Meals on Wheels can be a temporary means of providing for your nutritional needs when you are unable to shop and prepare food, or it can also be used as a long-term solution to this problem. Meals on Wheels is sponsored by most Visiting Nurse Associations throughout the country.

Old Talk *New Conversations*

Example #2: John

John, who lives alone, fell in the shower, hit his head, and managed to crawl to the telephone to call his daughter. After a hospital stay of six days, during which John was treated for a mild heart attack, concussion, and sprained hand, the doctor referred him to the hospital discharge planner. The discharge planner, John, and his daughter agreed that John could return home, but that he would not be able to go out for therapy until he had built up his strength, possibly over a month or six weeks. A home healthcare plan was prescribed by the physician consistent with the rules that make the services eligible for Medicare reimbursement. A licensed home health agency provided a physical therapist to visit the home for strengthening exercises, a nurse to monitor John's medications, and a home health aide for two hours a day for four to five days a week to assist with bathing and dressing. Meals on Wheels were also ordered, as was Lifeline, so that John can call for emergency help if he is alone and has new signs of a heart attack or some other change in his health status.

Adult day services are neighborhood programs located in churches, retirement communities, or freestanding centers that provide a safe place for you to go during the day so that your caregiver can go to work, shop, or simply have some time off from caregiving duties. These programs cost less (approximately $40/day) than hiring a private caregiver to stay in the home. They provide meals, social interaction, and, in some centers, bathing, therapy services, and even occasional weekend overnight care so that the caregiver can have time off (this is called respite care). Most of these centers also provide transportation.

You can also hire **paraprofessional aides, companions**, and **homemakers**, either privately yourself or through an agency. You will need to pay for this help yourself unless you have long-term care insurance that pays for in-home caregivers. If you hire your own aides, you should check at least two work-related references. You will need to carefully and fully explain what you expect the aide to do, and you also need to make sure that you pay all appropriate taxes and have the required insurance coverage. You can get information about taxes and insurance from your accountant.

Caregivers can also be arranged through an agency. While this may cost more per hour than hiring an aide yourself, hiring an agency assures you of coverage when the aide is sick, on vacation, or quits; and the agency also carries the liability insurance and pays the employment taxes. Most paraprofessional agencies also bond their employees, check police and driver's license records, and provide supervision. When you are trying to decide on an agency to hire, ask them how they handle employee cancellations, request references (unless the agency was referred to you by someone you trust who has used the agency), and find out how long the agency has been in business. You can also check on the agency with the local Better Business Bureau. The agency should provide you with a brochure and fee schedule, explaining how they provide their services and what the fees are, including how overtime and holidays are handled. Find out if the agency develops a written care plan that gives the aides specific instructions about what to do. Also ask about the agency's method of supervision of the caregivers.

Old Talk *New Conversations*

Example #3: Patrick and Mary

Patrick and Mary have lived in the same home for the 55 years they have been married. During the past six months it has become clear to Mary that Patrick's memory has become seriously impaired. In addition, he constantly gets up at night, sometimes to go to the toilet and sometimes to just wander all over the house, getting a snack, turning on the lights, and making it impossible for Mary to sleep. Sometimes Patrick is confused, and once he accused Mary of being a stranger.

Mary took Patrick to their family doctor, who recommended that a specialist examine Patrick. The specialist, a geriatric psychiatrist, diagnosed an Alzheimer's-type dementia. He prescribed several medications that seemed to help keep Patrick calm, but Mary is afraid to leave him in the home alone when she goes out. The couple's adult children are very attentive, but they have families and jobs.

Mary decided to hire a woman to stay with Patrick when she went out, and found a pleasant person through a neighbor. Unfortunately, the woman was constantly calling at the last minute to cancel. Someone told Mary about the Special Care Adult Day Center located in a church about five miles from their home. Mary was afraid that Patrick wouldn't want to go, since he was not an "arts-and-crafts" type of man, but the day center staff reassured Mary that there were many different types of activities. They reminded her that she needed to have a safe place for him while she shopped, spent time with a friend, or just had a chance to be home and take a nap without worrying about Patrick. To Mary's surprise, Patrick enjoys going to his "club," as he calls it.

Change, Loss, Grief, Mourning, Life Review and Renewals

Growing old is not for sissies! As you age, you are forced to confront a series of losses: minor losses—hair, waistline, energy—and major losses, such as the people you love. The sadness and grief you may feel is natural, and it is not easy to "get over it." For some people religious beliefs can help to soften the blows a long life has dealt them. Other people review their life story, write a memoir, organize their photos, or clean out their attics, carefully choosing objects important to them to give to their family or friends. These kinds of activities can help you come to a sense of fulfillment of a life spent as well as possible.

However, anger can overwhelm you, as can a numbing depression, dread, or anxiety. Depression and anxiety may actually be an organic illness that can be treated with mood-stabilizing medications. If you find that you are crying, or on the verge of crying, every day, or if you feel constantly angry and fearful, unable to name what upsets you, you can seek diagnosis and treatment from a geriatric psychiatrist, a medical specialist who can detect the difference between normal grief and clinical depression.

Many older people grew up with a mindset that you "tough out" your problems. They find it hard to believe that feelings are caused not only by life's circumstances but also by biochemical changes in the brain. A course of antidepressants or antianxiety medication, coupled with individual therapy for those willing to consider it, can significantly improve your outlook and your ability to handle day-to-day life.

You may find that your ability to accept the inevitable

changes and challenges of living a long life is helped by your recognition of how your children, family members, or friends are helping you. An important step is to choose a person to act as your **Healthcare Power of Attorney**. You need to discuss with the person you are designating for this role what you would want him or her to do if it is necessary to make healthcare decisions for you. For example, if it appeared that you were at the end of your life, would you want your Healthcare Power of Attorney to choose care the purpose which is to assure you are comfortable and pain-free, avoiding life-prolonging interventions? Having these discussions before they are needed will help insure that your wishes are followed if you become unable to make your opinions known yourself.

What If You Can No Longer Make Your Own Decisions?

Sometimes a family wonders if the older person is still able to make his or her own decisions. They may have noticed changes in the person's behavior, appearance, physical health, daily routine, or eating habits. A simple way to assess someone's **decision-making capacit**y is to ask yourself questions such as: has the person lost any substantial amount of weight in the past six to eight months? Does he keep appointments you have made with him? Is the household upkeep the way it has always been? Does the person call you or someone else frequently, asking the same questions? Has his personal grooming deteriorated?

If you observe important changes in these areas of personal care, memory, and thinking, you can then ask yourself: if this individual faced an important decision to make, could she comprehend the facts she would need to consider to make the decision? Can she deliberate about the facts in a manner that is consistent with her own past practices? Can she communicate any decisions she has to make to you?

If the individual does not seem to be able to comprehend the facts of decisions she needs to make, or if she seems to be making decisions that are inconsistent with similar decisions she has made in the past, you should arrange for a professional assessment by a physician or psychologist. Healthcare decision-making passes to the person who has been identified as the Healthcare Power of Attorney when two physicians, or a physician and a psychologist, examine the individual and state in writing that the person is unable to receive and evaluate information effectively or to communicate decisions to the extent that the person lacks the capacity to manage his or her healthcare decisions.

Example #4: The Rogers Family

The Rogers family was distraught at a meeting with a social worker to discuss what to do about their mother. Mrs. Rogers was in the hospital, having had a mild stroke. The discharge planner had told the son and daughter that their mother was ready to leave the hospital, but she lived alone, and the adult children could not agree on whether she should return home. The daughter, who spoke to her mother daily, thought she was "getting senile," since her mother recently had begun to repeat herself and couldn't seem to remember appointments they had arranged. The son thought his mother was fine and could get along with just a little more help, which he was willing to provide. Neither of the children had asked their mother what she wanted to do. The social worker recommended that the children request that a geriatric psychiatrist examine their mother before she left the hospital to help them decide if she was able to make her own healthcare decisions.

After examining Mrs. Rogers, the psychiatrist and social worker met with the whole family. The psychiatrist explained that the memory and thinking problems that the daughter had observed might have been caused by her acute illness. While she had some loss of mental functioning, Mrs. Rogers was still capable of making decisions for herself. The social worker explained the purpose of a Healthcare Power of Attorney and Mrs. Rogers signed the form the social worker brought. Mrs. Rogers expressed relief that she had now arranged for her son and daughter to make healthcare decisions for her if she could no longer make these decisions for herself in the future.

The family agreed that it would be helpful to have an agency provide Mrs. Rogers with some home care so that her daughter did not feel overwhelmed. Since Mrs. Rogers lived in an apartment near a shopping center and with no steps to climb, she could return home safely with a raised toilet seat, a shower chair, and bars installed in the tub. Her son agreed to help her balance her checkbook, and her daughter agreed to do the food shopping each week. The Rogers family left the conference feeling that they had a workable home-care plan with which everyone was comfortable.

CHAPTER FIVE

CHOOSING YOUR NEW HOME: RETIREMENT/SENIOR HOUSING

BY MATT FURNO, NHA

One of the milestones most people face as they grow older is planning their senior years. This process involves many factors, including the decision of whether to remain in your current dwelling and receive home-based care or to move into a retirement community.

This decision is difficult and does not have a "one-size-fits-all" solution. The best answers are multifaceted and uniquely driven by what meets the needs and desires of each individual. Some of the issues affecting the decision include health issues, activity level, safety, support base, well-being, and finances.

First, it is of paramount importance that the final decision be made by you, not your children, relatives, or friends. Also, you must allow adequate time to prevent a sense of being rushed during the decision-making process.

Finally, decisions of this magnitude should never be attempted immediately following the death of a spouse. You should wait at least one year after the death of a loved one before deciding on housing options. Depression is common in the senior population—its intensity and duration can be lessened by allowing time to heal.

This chapter will assist you in making your senior planning decisions by helping you understand the complexities of choosing a retirement community that is right for you. The right choice will provide an environment that will be safe and affordable and will encourage you to live life to the fullest.

Determining In-Home Care Versus a Retirement Community

During the initial decision-making process it is necessary to decide which aspects of your life are most important, such as safety, socialization, or health status. Next, determine where these aspects are best fulfilled, in your home or at a retirement community. Be as objective and creative as possible during this process.

When choosing between home care and a retirement community, there are many factors to be considered. Every individual has a different lifestyle, which makes each person's decision unique. The following sections provide an outline of the issues to consider when exploring your personal options.

Loneliness. The constant commotion of family is something many people miss as they age or as their children move away. The loss of a loved one may find you living alone for the first time in your life.

It is important to consider the social aspect of housing when determining where you will live. Having visitors or family involvement is very important emotionally.

Individual activity levels and support systems are also important factors in preventing loneliness. For some people being in a retirement community with other seniors is a perfect environment for increased happiness.

Example # 1: Emily

Emily is 71 years old. She has raised four children and always had a house full of people. Two years ago her husband passed away, and she found herself living alone in their large home. After much research Emily decided to move to an independent retirement community. She has her own apartment with all her furnishings, plus she has the companionship and daily activities available in a community setting.

Convenient access to transportation can also reduce loneliness. Without the ability to get out of the house regularly, or to participate in desired activities, you may become isolated and lonely. Routine tasks such as grocery shopping may become difficult. Retirement communities can provide assistance with these tasks.

Health Status. Another important factor to consider in determining where you live is your health status. If health issues or special assistance are a concern, you must determine where the services you need can most appropriately be provided, at home or in a retirement community.

There are many levels of health to consider. For some seniors assistance is only needed in daily living activities such as bathing, preparing meals, or maintaining medication. For others more care is needed.

OldTalk New Conversations

Example # 2: Howard

Howard, 77 years old, has diabetes and needs assistance with his daily medication. He has decided to move into an assisted living facility that allows him to live independently, yet receive assistance with his medication and daily meals.

Other important factors when deciding on home care versus a retirement community include activities of daily living, such as balancing a checkbook, paying bills, shopping, and exercising.

Example # 3: Kathleen

Kathleen is 81 years old. She is active but could not handle heavy housework such as vacuuming or raking. She needed assistance maintaining her home. She decided to remain in her home and find a home care agency to help her with heavy duties.

A health setback such as surgery or a broken bone may require temporary special care. Rehabilitation services provide the physical therapy and special care to help you return safely home.

Example # 4: Matthew

Matthew, 68 years old, fell on an ice patch and broke his hip. Following surgery, he entered a skilled nursing rehabilitation facility that allowed him to recuperate and provided daily therapy to increase his mobility. Once he was back on his feet, he returned home.

If you have a special medical condition, you need to explore the options available for making life enjoyable and safe. There are many options designed to care for special needs such as Alzheimer's disease, dementia, and other chronic illnesses. Community-Based Residential Facilities (CBRF) or skilled nursing facilities can provide this specialized care.

Safe Environment. Safety is another important issue to consider. If you have trouble driving, shoveling snow, or climbing stairs, these factors should be considered when determining where to live. Neighborhood safety should also be a consideration when deciding on in-home services versus relocation.

Socialization. Living life to the fullest and being able to participate in activities you enjoy is very important. When determining where to live, you must define the activities that give meaning to your life and provide a sense of self-worth.

Example # 5: Ellen

Ellen is 82 years old and has volunteered at the veterans' hospital for 24 years. Because of her love for helping others, she chose a senior community with a continuum of care. This has allowed her to live independently in an apartment and continue volunteering at the rehabilitation center.

Mobility. Mobility is another important factor in the decision-making process. Most houses are not user friendly, especially if you have special needs such as a wheelchair. It is important to determine how restrictions in your current setting, such as a laundry room in the basement or a bathroom with difficult shower access, limit your accessibility.

Old Talk New Conversations

Financial Concerns. One of the most difficult questions people ask is, "How do I plan my retirement with the money that I have?" Unfortunately, there is not a magic formula everyone can use. Rather, it is important that all factors be considered and a budget be determined that fits into each individual's finances. (Chapters One and Three go into this in greater detail.)

Once you have decided whether to choose home care or a retirement community, a thorough search should be conducted to find services that fit into your specific budget.

If you plan to remain in your home, it is important to plan for the costs associated with a house, such as property taxes and general maintenance. Overall the decision to stay in a house requires researching the home health assistance available from family and friends as well as through home care services in the community. (Chapter Four goes into this in greater detail.)

If you choose to move into a retirement community, you must determine what services you require and research what the facilities in your community have to offer. Retirement communities come with a wide range of services, which are discussed later in this chapter.

You've Decided on a Retirement Community . . . But Where?

Once you have decided to move into a retirement community, it is important to understand all the options available. Senior living is not what it used to be! The needs of an active senior population have been met with a variety of choices in housing, from senior condominiums and apartments to assisted living and skilled nursing facilities. As the population over age 65 continues to grow, the options in senior living continue to expand.

Understanding the full range of options and developing a complete list of your needs will help define the environment that is best suited for your new home.

The Scope of Retirement Communities. The fact that there are more choices for seniors today than just a few short years ago allows you to select a home that best matches your needs. It also can make choosing the right facility much more difficult. The following defines the different facility options and categorizes them according to the amenities and services they offer.

Continuum of Care. This term refers to the full scope of care available. It is used for communities that have the ability to take care of seniors at any level of need in different facilities on one campus.

Independent Senior Living. This refers to complexes that provide apartments or condominiums for rent or ownership to seniors only. These facilities do not provide health assistance, but they may offer amenities such as housekeeping, laundry, parking, meals, and recreational/social activities.

Continuing Care Retirement Community (CCRC). These communities are usually designed in a campus environment and offer options of care, ranging from independent living to assisted living and skilled nursing. These communities offer seniors the security of being able to age in place without having to move if their health deteriorates.

OldTalk *New Conversations*

Community-Based Residential Facility (CBRF). These facilities are licensed by the State of Wisconsin and provide intermediate care, which includes meals, recreation, and housekeeping services. The facility can provide no more than three hours of skilled nursing care a week.

Residential Care Apartment Complex (RCAC). These facilities are commonly referred to as "assisted living" facilities because they offer apartments with kitchens and baths, but provide services to assist in daily living. Services at a RCAC include medication management, personal care assistance, housekeeping, and meal preparation. They can provide services on an as-needed basis and emergency service 24 hours a day. The concept is to allow you to choose those services necessary and add others as the need arises. In Wisconsin, these facilities are licensed by the State for up to 28 hours per week of services, including supportive, personal, and nursing care. You must be capable of independent living to enter a RCAC.

Intermediate Care Facility (ICF). An ICF provides intermediate nursing care consisting of physical, emotional, social, and other rehabilitative services with medical supervision. Most seniors at these facilities need ongoing assistance with a long-term illness or a disability that has reached a plateau. These facilities are licensed by the State of Wisconsin.

Skilled Nursing Facility (SNF). Skilled nursing facilities are licensed by the State of Wisconsin to provide skilled nursing services for patients with either a short-term rehabilitation need following hospitalization or for patients with a need for long-term care. Skilled nursing services means those services provided under a physician's order.

Developing a Personal Needs Chart for Choosing a Retirement Community

Prior to searching out retirement community options, it is best to assess your individual needs and wants. Every person has different lifestyle needs that, when defined, will assist him or her in determining the facility that will be the best match.

The following outlines three important areas to assess. Determine your individual criteria and develop a chart of the services, amenities, and activities that you want in a retirement community. By developing this Personal Needs Chart, you will be able to narrow your options and focus your efforts on the communities that match your specific needs.

Personal Assessment. To begin, conduct a personal needs assessment. Determine the things that you will need assistance with, as well as the things you plan to continue to take care of yourself.

Physical—Physical needs range from the ability to climb stairs to wheel chair accessibility, depending upon your physical condition. Your physical limitations should be determined as well as the things that would make those limitations easier.

Old Talk New Conversations

Example # 5: John

John is 84 years old. He fell and broke his hip and could no longer walk without assistance. John moved to an assisted living facility that provided nursing care and some assistance with daily living so he could live independently.

Mental—Mental capacity is an important issue to discuss when determining the best living situation. It is natural to get more forgetful with age. For most of us forgetfulness is just a result of our busy lives. But for some it is a serious problem that can be dangerous if living alone. Good communication with your physician and an openness with those assisting with the decision-making process should help provide direction as to your particular needs.

Example # 6: Harriet

Harriet is 92 years old. She had maintained her home for many years but became more forgetful and needed assistance. Cooking had become dangerous. Harriet decided to move to an assisted living facility where she has her own apartment but is provided meals in the dining room, a daily check for safety, and other assistance when necessary.

Emotional—Happiness is an important factor in determining where to live. The loss of a loved one can leave you feeling alone and afraid. It is important that issues such as companionship and socialization be considered as part of the decision-making process.

Example # 7: Margaret

Margaret is 71 years old. She lost her husband and felt overwhelmed with the care of their large home. She was also afraid and lonely being there by herself. Her family wanted to help, but they lived far away. Margaret chose an independent living facility where she could have her own apartment, the security she wanted, and the companionship of people her own age.

Psychological—Examine your feelings about retirement communities and where you see yourself being most happy. Match your personality and lifestyle to the culture of the community. Do the people living in the community share common bonds with you, such as religion, income level, social status, and interests? What things are most important to your lifestyle environment?

Lifestyle Assessment. An integral part of happiness is the accessibility to those things you enjoy. Whether it is woodworking, playing cards, long walks, or golfing, be sure that your living choice provides those activities. Although you may not find an environment that offers everything, those lifestyle issues that are most important should be maintained. This assessment should include all areas of lifestyle such as:

- Recreation activities such as woodworking, golf, crafts
- Proximity to those you want to see
- Housekeeping
- Work/volunteer commitments
- Organizational involvement in the community

Old Talk New Conversations

Develop a list of those things that must be available or accessible from your new home as well as those that would be nice but are not essential.

Financial Assessment. The finances for senior planning are perhaps the most individual decision of all. You need to match the list of services, amenities, and activities with your ability to pay. The "Financial Structure" section later in this chapter lists some of the questions to ask when matching your financial ability with the services of a facility.

In Search of the Most Appropriate Facility

Once your assessment has been made, you are ready to determine which retirement community is best suited to you. The rest of this chapter deals with the process of choosing a retirement community and how to get the most out of your new home.

Step One: Research. Now that you have developed a chart of services, amenities, and activities, you can explore different retirement communities. Perhaps the most important factor is determining the appropriate geographic location. Is it in your current community? Is it near a relative or loved one? Are you willing to move to a new location altogether?

Once you have chosen a specific area, contact the available facilities for informational literature. It is important to make notes as you talk with representatives from each community. To avoid a heavy "sales pitch," inform the representative that you are in the process of researching all the area facilities and will contact those you are interested in touring at a later date.

Once you receive the literature, take the time to read it and outline the services and amenities each community offers. This will help determine which communities you want to visit. Choose the top communities that fit your needs and arrange a tour and fact-finding meeting.

During the entire selection process individual tradeoffs will probably need to be made. It is important to prioritize your needs and desires. No one community will offer everything you want, but it should meet your most important criteria.

Step Two: Evaluating the Retirement Community. Once you have chosen those communities that meet your requirements, schedule a tour and fact-finding meeting with each facility. Develop a sheet of notes for each tour and fill in the answers as you go. You may want to take a family member or friend along on your tour to gain another perspective and to assist you in the final decision. The following are key areas to address during the tour.

First Impression—Your first impression of a retirement community is very important. Remember, this could be your new home, and how you are greeted today is indicative of how you will be greeted for many years to come.

When looking at different facilities, you should expect to be treated with respect and provided all the information you ask for. Your first impression should be a good one.

As you enter a new facility, evaluate the physical environment and the congeniality of the staff and residents. It should give you a homey, comfortable feeling. Feel free to explain that you are

Old Talk New Conversations

touring the facility, and talk with the staff and residents about the amenities, services, and general culture of the community.

Organizational History and Operating Philosophy—Experience in delivering senior services is important. Check on the longevity of the organization and its experience/history. Usually states license and accredit facilities on an annual basis. Ask for the results of that survey and their accreditation history. Ask if the facility has been sited for problems, and have each incident explained thoroughly.

Environmental Considerations—The overall appearance of the retirement community is very important. Observe the general maintenance of the exterior and interior of the building. Check the condition of the furnishings, the overall cleanliness of the campus, and any observable odors throughout the building. If you have concerns, do not hesitate to question the representative. You should approach this as you approached buying a home and feel free to ask questions.

It is important to also consider the culture of the campus. Is it inviting, pleasant, and safe? What does the surrounding neighborhood look like? Do residents and staff appear pleasant and outgoing? You should be proud to invite guests to visit your new home and your new "neighbors."

Staffing—Each facility will have staff members in a variety of positions to manage the services provided. It is important to understand how these people are hired and retained as well as the specific expectations of their job. Be sure to note the attitudes and appearance of staff members during your tour. Here are a few questions to ask each facility:

- What is the ratio of staff to resident?
- What is the turnover rate (average length of service) for direct and indirect care staff?
- What qualifications are required of direct care staff?
- What is the level of volunteer interaction with residents?

Location—The location of your new home should be taken into consideration. It should be convenient for family and friends to visit. Check if there is ample visitor parking and guest rooms for overnight stays.

Convenience is just as important for you. If you want to be active in the community, is your new home in a convenient location for getting where you want to go? Check the vicinity for bus routes or for parking if you want a car. Does the facility provide transportation to residents? Are there services nearby such as restaurants, shopping, or a park? All the things that you enjoy should be accessible from your new home.

Housing—As mentioned earlier, many facilities offer a continuum of care, from independent homes to skilled nursing care. This allows residents the opportunity to age in place and be cared for as their needs change. You will want to discuss the different housing options available at each facility and identify the type of service that fits your needs best.

Tour all the different housing options, even if you currently do not need extensive care. This will help you gauge how the facility handles the healthcare or assistance needs you may have

Old Talk *New Conversations*

in the future.

As you tour the area of the community in which you will live, ask very direct questions about occupancy and living arrangements. Discuss the extent to which you can personalize the unit, such as overall color, carpet or hard floors, window treatments, and structural modification. Many places allow you to bring your own furniture, paintings, and other belongings. Note the size, cost, and layout of the different units available and find out exact occupancy dates.

If the facility offers skilled nursing care, discuss whether they offer private or semiprivate rooms and what kind of healthcare and rehabilitation services are offered.

Example # 8: Jeanette

Jeanette is 83 years old. She fell and broke her hip and needed to move from her apartment to the facility's skilled nursing unit during her recovery. The facility held her apartment while she recuperated, and she was able to get back to her home in six weeks.

Professional Services on Campus—One benefit to living in a retirement community is the on-site services that are available, especially professional services. Depending upon your specific needs, it is important to examine the services available and discuss how each service would be provided to you.

The following list of services should be examined as you look for a new home:
- Medical (physicians and associated staff)
- Dental (dentists and dental staff)
- Podiatry

- Audiology
- Therapy (physical, occupational, speech, and respiratory)
- Emergency
- Pharmacy
- Nutrition (dietitian)

Beyond those services on-site it is important to understand the availability of services in the area. The distance to the hospital, the emergency department, outpatient services, and a medical arts building (physicians' offices and clinics) are just some of the issues that should be explored.

Amenities—The amenities of a facility are very important in maintaining your lifestyle. If you enjoy woodworking, for example, make sure to visit the craft and woodworking shop.

There are many amenities that a facility may offer. Here is a list of on-site amenities to consider:

- Wellness, exercise, and aquatic facilities
- Gift shop and/or convenience store
- Beauty and barber shops
- Dental office
- Bank
- Postal services
- Library
- Computer and Internet access
- Security system
- Valet services
- Vault for storage of valuables
- Guest rooms and services
- Gardening plots
- Masseuse
- Educational opportunities

OldTalk New Conversations

You will also want to know about policies regarding:
- Smoking
- Pets
- Visitor hours
- Visitor eating and living accommodations
- Resident job program
- Resident volunteer program

Transportation—Many seniors are busy with active lifestyles that demand transportation. Determine what each facility offers, such as parking for your car or facility transportation services. Here are some things to inquire about:
- Parking availability for personal vehicle—surface versus garaged space
- Facility transportation availability and cost for transport to medical and dental appointments, recreational activities, or personal excursions

Activities—Because the activities of the retirement community should match your interests, it is important to understand and visit the different activity areas in each facility. A retirement community may list woodworking classes on its activity sheet, but one facility may have a fully equipped woodworking shop that outshines the competition.

Community activities are another important factor. Request to see copies of the activity department's calendar of events for the past three months. Explore what is offered on campus, such as entertainment, holiday events, cookouts, hands-on recreational activities, educational presentations, and worship services.

Ask about the facilities used for events (party rooms, auditorium, theater) and ask to tour each area. The kinds of facilities that a community has can determine the extent of their on-campus events.

Next, request information about off-campus events. If you enjoy the symphony, for example, make sure that your new community offers this type of recreational outing. The facility representative should be able to provide a list of events that have been available in the past three months, such as sports outings, shopping trips, sightseeing tours, field trips, educational lectures, and restaurant dining experiences.

Dining Services—An important aspect of any retirement facility is the dining accommodations. There are many different options for dining depending upon the facility you choose. For apartment facilities the dining may be limited, while in skilled nursing facilities all meals are prepared.

To better understand the services of the facility you are touring, use the following checklist:

- Number of dining locations and appearance
- Variety of sizes of dining rooms
- Delivery of food services to apartment/room
- Availability of private dining
- Menu
    - Frequency or rotation cycle of items on the menu
    - Daily choices
    - Extent of menu offerings at each meal
    - Availability of healthy choices at each meal
    - Availability of guest menus
    - Policy and procedure for special orders
    - Policy and procedure for following special diets

OldTalk New Conversations

While you are on the tour, request to sample the food. The timing of your tour could be set up to include lunch. This will give you a good opportunity to see the dining area and sample the food, as well as sit down with the representative to discuss any unanswered questions.

Check the food for presentation, taste, portions, and quality. Does it taste homemade and offer a good selection? Is there freshness and variety?

Religious Services—Some facilities are associated with a specific religious order, while others are nondenominational. For those not affiliated with a particular religion, check to see if they provide a schedule of religious services to meet your needs. Many facilities have a chaplain on staff or are associated with local clergy who can take care of personal needs. Also, ask to tour the chapel or meditation room.

Ancillary Services—Housekeeping and laundry are two tasks that many people are eager to give up, so be sure to discuss the availability of these services.

- Housekeeping services
    - Frequency
    - Extent
    - Cost
- Laundry services
    - Frequency
    - Location of drop-off and pick-up versus delivery to room
    - Cost

Financial Structure—The cost of your new home is vitally important to the decision-making process. This information should be provided in a clear, concise way that is easy to understand. If you are confused about any aspect of the payment process, feel free to ask questions and get further information. To get added perspective, discuss the finances of your new home with a family member, friend, or your accountant.

In determining the costs of your new home, ask the facility representative to provide clear pricing sheets that describe what is included and what is priced individually. This will help you determine a monthly budget. The following outlines some of the areas to cover:

- Base price: what does it include?
- Fee schedule
- Participation with governmental reimbursement programs
- Participation with third-party reimbursement programs
- History of fee increases: frequency and percent
- Variety of fee packages: do they have lifecare?
- What happens if your present financial status changes?

Transferring through the Continuum—If you are entering a facility for reasons other than health, it is important to understand the services available should your health status change. Many facilities offer a continuum of care on their campus and can accommodate your needs should they arise. It is important to understand how to access services as your needs change

Old Talk *New Conversations*

Other General Questions:
- What is the access to management during off hours?
- Is there a safety system in place to verify the well-being of each person on a daily basis?
- What is the complaint procedure and how are complaints handled?
- Does the service staff utilize a team approach?
- Are family members updated (via telephone calls, letters, and/or in person) according to the resident's desires?
- Are family members invited to attend care-plan sessions?
- How active is the resident council?
- What is the frequency of resident and family meetings?
- What reasons and sequence of events have been cited for evictions of residents?
- What is the organizational mission statement and purpose?

Step 3: The Final Decision. Spend at least a weekend at the facility of your choice before making a final decision. Most organizations provide accommodations, some at no cost, that will allow you to experience the community. This should give you a full understanding of the facility, allow you to meet some of the people in your new community, and help you make your decision.

Relocation . . . The Move

Moving is always a hectic experience, so try to make the move as enjoyable as you can. Give yourself plenty of time to move into your new home and get as much help as possible. Be sure to include your family or members of your support group in your move.

In many facilities you can bring as much of your own furniture and furnishings as will fit. To make your new home feel like home, bring the items you want, including photos, paintings and other decorative items. Allow yourself some adjustment time before disposing of your remaining furnishings. You may find that once you are in your new home, there is something else you have that would fit in perfectly.

Optimizing Your Lifestyle within the System. Attitude, attitude, attitude! Getting the most out of your new home depends a lot upon you. It is important to approach your move as a new adventure, one of making your new home feel like home.

Meet the decision makers in your new environment very early. Their titles vary, but by requesting an organizational chart, you can easily ascertain what level of management addresses a particular concern.

These key management people will be advocates for you if there are areas in your new home that are not to your satisfaction. A good rule of thumb: it is most beneficial to follow the chain of command starting at the lowest point and then move upward if a satisfactory result has not been accomplished.

Periodically request a dinner engagement with a member of the top management staff. Often more insight and persuasion can occur during a dining experience than a confrontational meeting.

Most important, become involved. Most facilities have a residential council that assists in making decisions for the facility. There are also many activity planning committees and other community areas that need assistance. By participating in these groups, you will have influence on the culture of your new community.

Old Talk New Conversations

Retirement communities have come a long way from the homes that served the last generation. Finding a community that provides for your needs and accommodates your interests will add to your happiness and fulfillment.

POSTSCRIPT
FROM THE AUTHORS

◆

Now that you have read this book, what is the next step? If you are the adult child, the niece or nephew, the close friend, or neighbor of someone with whom you would like to start the "new conversations" addressed in this book, how do you get started?

If the older person is over 80, you may be surprised to find that he or she is relieved to have you broach these subjects. If the person is younger, you may, at least initially, be more likely to get a mixed reaction. You could give our book as a "stocking stuffer" or a Grandparents' Day or Mother's or Father's Day present. Or start with the "Roadmap For Heirs" on page 26, since it just lists the factual information most people would want their family or close friends to know about them. Or consider whether your church or synagogue could host an informal discussion group centered on these issues.

Some families are very straightforward and willing to talk candidly about these issues. A direct approach explaining why you want to discuss these subjects works if this is the style of communication in your family.

Other families are more circumspect, and rarely talk about difficult or potentially unpleasant subjects. In some families there may be one child who is particularly suited to discuss the family's

OldTalk New Conversations

finances, while another is best able to discuss the type of care plans the parents would prefer. Sometimes these conversations can be started more easily by a son, sometimes by a daughter.

Often the family member who lives closest is able to bring up these subjects, but sometimes the one who lives the furthest away is the best person for the job. Regardless of who assumes which role, remember that OldTalk flourishes under a Golden Rule umbrella: a gentle, respectful attitude and a readiness to listen as well as to talk can work wonders.

It might help if the adult children meet first to discuss their concerns and decide on how to approach their parents. Often it is best to avoid involving the in-laws, although if an in-law has particular expertise that the parents respect (for example, a nurse or a lawyer), that in-law might be successful in speaking to the parents. Sometimes it is wise to consult with a geriatric care manager or an attorney specializing in trust and estate work, or suggest such a consultation to your parents. Adult children who have tended to their own planning needs, for example with a financial planner and/or attorney, can use their own considerations as a way to open up the conversation.

However you are able, we hope *OldTalk:New Conversations* will help you and your family today.

AUTHOR PROFILES

◆

Phyllis Mensh Brostoff, ACSW, CISW

Matt Furno, NHA

John A. Herbers, JD

Paula H. Hogan, CFP, CFA

Steven J. Koppel, CLU, ChFC

Author Profiles

Paula H. Hogan
Hogan Financial Management
250 W. Coventry Ct. #210
Milwaukee, WI 53217
414-352-9111
hogan@hoganfinancial.com
www.hoganfinancial.com

Paula H. Hogan is the founder of Hogan Financial Management, a firm that has been providing comprehensive, fee-only financial planning and portfolio management services since 1992. Paula is a past President of the Wisconsin Chapter of the American Association of Individual Investors and now serves on the National Board of NAPFA (National Association of Personal Financial Advisors) as chair of the Ethics Committee. In 1998 *Medical Economics* magazine listed Paula as one of the 120 best financial advisors for doctors. Paula has earned both the Chartered Financial Analyst (1986) and Certified Financial Planner (1986) designations as well as an A.B. cum laude from Princeton University in economics (1975) and an M.S. from Harvard University (1978).

John A. Herbers
Reinhart, Boerner, et al.
1000 N. Water St. #2100
Milwaukee, WI 53202
414-298-8176
jherbers@reinhartlaw.com
www.reinhartlaw.com

John A. Herbers has been an attorney since 1982 and is currently a shareholder with Reinhart, Boerner, Van Deuren, Norris & Rieselbach, s.c., in Milwaukee. He has written and lectured extensively, nationally and locally, on a wide variety of estate planning issues, including retirement income planning and the specialized planning required for owners and managers of family-owned businesses. John is licensed to practice law in both Wisconsin and Florida, and is a member of the Real Property, Probate and Trust Law Section of the American Bar Association. He is also a Fellow of the American College of Trust and Estate Counsel. He is a graduate cum laude of Boston College Law School (1982) and Georgetown University (1979).

Steven J. Koppel
Northwestern Mutual Life
1101 N. Market St. #100
Milwaukee, WI 53202
414-615-1810
steven.koppel@nml.com
www.northwesternmutual.com

Steven J. Koppel founded his insurance practice in 1978 and is past President of the Milwaukee Chapter of the Society of Financial Service Professionals and the Estate Counselors Forum of Milwaukee. He is a life and qualifying member of the Million Dollar Round Table. Steve is an agent associated with the Schwertfeger General Agency of the Northwestern Mutual Life Insurance Company in Milwaukee, Wisconsin, and an agent of the Northwestern Long Term Care Insurance Company, a subsidiary of Northwestern Mutual Life. Steve received a B.A. in Political Science from American University (1973) and a J.D. from Ohio Northern University School of Law (1976).

Phyllis Mensh Brostoff has specialized in geriatric care issues for over 25 years. She is currently Cofounder and President of Stowell Associates, Inc. and SelectStaff Services, Inc. Stowell Associates, founded in 1983, is a private geriatric care management company. SelectStaff Services, founded in 1996, provides housekeepers, companions, and personal care aides to elderly and disabled adults. Phyllis has taught social work and aging courses at the School of Social Welfare, University of Wisconsin-Milwaukee; was a Cofounder and past Treasurer of the National Association of Professional Geriatric Care Managers; and has given numerous speeches and presentations, locally and nationally, on aging issues and social work ethics. She has an M.S.W. from the University of Maryland-Baltimore (1970) and a B.A. in English literature from George Washington University, Washington, D.C. (1966).

PHYLLIS MENSH BROSTOFF
STOWELL ASSOCIATES/SELECT STAFF
4433 N. OAKLAND AVE.
414-962-3737
MILWAUKEE, WI 53211
select@mail.gmtcom.com
www.elderselectstaff.com

Matt Furno is a licensed nursing home administrator with over 25 years of experience in health care. He has been President/CEO at Milwaukee Protestant Home/Bradford Terrace since April 1997. Prior to that he served for nine years as Administrator of Orchard Manor in Lancaster, Wisconsin, a skilled nursing facility with an intermediate care facility for the mentally retarded. Matt received an M.S. in management from the University of Wisconsin-Milwaukee (1979), and a B.S. in bioenvironmental engineering (1974) and an associate degree in applied science in electronics (1973), both from the Milwaukee School of Engineering.

MATT FURNO
MILWAUKEE PROTESTANT HOME
2449 N. DOWNER AVE.
MILWAUKEE, WI 53211
414-332-8610
mphceo@execpc.com

INDEX

activities of daily living (ADL), 57–58
acute illness, 51–52
ADL (activities of daily living), 57–58
adult day services, 74, 76
aging of population, 49, 50 (chart)
aides, paraprofessional, 75
Alzheimer's Disease, 52–53
A.M. Best, 16, 64 (chart)
annuities, 37
antibiotics, 71–72
anxiety, 77
assessing decision-making
    capacity, 78-79
assisted living facilities, 51, 87–88
attorney-in-fact, 31.
    See also power of attorney

balance sheet for financial planning,
    6, 8–9 (illus.), 10
beneficiary designations, 24, 37
Best (A.M.), 16, 64 (chart)
bonds, 6, 14
Brostoff, Phyllis Mensh, 3, 109
burial, prearrangements for, 28

capital gains, 11, 39–40
care management, 68–70
cash flow, 10–11, 12–13 (illus.),
    16, 17–18
cash reserves (emergency reserves),
    6, 10
CBRF (community-based residential
    facility), 51, 88

CCRC (continuing care retirement
    communities), 87
Certificates of Deposit, 6–7
Chartered Life Underwriter (CLU), 65
chronic illness, 52
CLU (Chartered Life Underwriter), 65
commitments to new endeavors, 25
communication within the family, 3–4,
    23, 67–68, 105–106
community-based residential facility
    (CBRF), 51, 88
conservatorship, 30
continuing care retirement
    communities (CCRC), 87
corporations, as property management
    vehicles, 33
custodial care, 18, 20–21, 28

day care for adults, 74, 76
death
    coping with, 71–72
    spousal death, 81–82, 90–91
death certificate, data for, 28
debt management, 7, 10
decision-making capacity, 78–80
Declaration to Physicians
    (Living Will), 32
deferred compensation, 12 (illus.)
dementia, 52–53
depression, 77, 82
disability. *See* incapacity
discussing issues within the family,
    3–4, 23, 67–68, 105–106

110

Duff & Phelps, 64 (chart)
Durable Power of Attorney, 23–24, 31

earned income, 12 (illus.), 17
emergency reserves (cash reserves), 6, 10
emergency response system (lifeline), 73
emotional needs, 25, 90–91
estate planning, 2, 23–24, 29–39.
  See also taxes
  conservatorship, 30
  Declaration to Physicians, 32
  disability, planning for.
    See incapacity
  Durable Power of Attorney, 31
  Healthcare Power of Attorney, 31–32
  joint ownership, 32–33, 36
  joint trust, 43, 44 (chart)
  legal guardianship, 30
  living trust, 33, 35–36, 38, 39
  nonprobate transfers of assets, 33, 34, 35–39
  partnerships/corporations/limited liability companies, 33
  probate transfers of assets, 33–35
  revocable trust, 38, 39, 43, 45 (chart)
  Road Map for Heirs, 24, 26–28 (illus.)
estate tax, 41–43, 42 (chart), 44–45 (charts)
expenses, 12–13 (illus.)

family communication, 3–4, 25, 67–68, 105–106
family gifts to adult children, 12 (illus.), 22–23

family structure, changes in, 50, 67–68
financial planning for retirement, 2, 5–28. *See also* incapacity; investments; long-term care insurance
  balance sheet, 6, 8–9 (illus.), 10
  cash flow, 10–11, 12–13 (illus.), 16, 17–18
  commitments to new endeavors, 25
  health insurance, 16
  Heirs, Road Map for, 26–28 (illus.)
  inheritances, 22–24
  liabilities, 7, 9 (illus.)
  liquid assets, 6–7, 8 (illus.)
  personal property, 7, 9 (illus.), 10
  questions to ask, 5–6
  tax planning, 15–16
funeral, prearrangements for, 28
Furno, Matt, 3, 109

geriatric care management, 68–70
gifts to adult children, 12 (illus.), 22–23
gift tax, 40, 41 (chart)
government benefits, 49

Healthcare Power of Attorney, 31–32, 78, 79, 80
health insurance, 16
Health Insurance Portability and Accountability Act (1996), 57
health status, 83–85.
  See also incapacity
heirs, 26–28 (illus.), 34.
  See also inheritances
Herbers, John A., 2, 108
Hogan, Paula H., 2, 108

home healthcare, 67–80
  in a care facility versus at home, 51, 58
  and change/loss/grief, 77–78
  and decision-making capacity, 78–80
  decision-making process for, 68–70
  home-delivered meals, 73
  hospice care, 71–72
  licensed services, 70–71
  unlicensed services, 73–76
home living, 3, 19.
  See also home healthcare
  demographics of, 68
  finances for, 86
  and health status, 83–85
  and loneliness, 82–83
  and mobility, 85
  versus retirement community, 82–86
  and safety, 85
  and socialization, 85
hospice care, 71–72

ICF (intermediate care facility), 88
illness, acute versus chronic, 51–52
incapacity, 18–22, 24.
  See also long-term care insurance
  acute versus chronic illness, 51–52
  conservatorship, 30
  Declaration to Physicians, 32
  Durable Power of Attorney, 31
  Healthcare Power of Attorney, 31–32, 78
  for home healthcare decisions, 78–80
  joint ownership, 32–33, 36
  legal guardianship, 30
  living trust, 33, 35–36, 38, 39

  partnerships/corporations/limited liability companies, 33
  planning for, 29–33
income, 12 (illus.)
income tax, 39–40
independent senior living, 87
inflation, 11, 60
inheritances, 22–24, 39.
insurance.
  See also long-term care insurance
  beneficiary designations for policies, 37
  costs of, 12 (illus.)
  health insurance, 16
  insurance company ratings, 16, 62–63, 64 (chart)
  loans on policies, 10
  and peace of mind, 55–56
interest/dividends, 11
intermediate care facility (ICF), 88
intestacy laws, 34
investments, 7, 8–9 (illus.), 10, 12 (illus.), 15–16
IRAs, 37

joint ownership, 32–33, 36
joint trust, 43, 44 (chart)

Kennedy-Kassenbaum Bill (1996), 57
Koppel, Steven J., 2–3, 108

legal guardianship, 30
liabilities, 7, 9 (illus.)
life estate deeds, 36–37
life expectancy, 6, 47–48
Lifeline, 73

lifestyle assessment, 91–92
life tenant, 36
limited liability companies, 33
liquid assets, 6–7, 8 (illus.)
Living Revocable Trust, 38, 39
living trust, 33, 35–36, 38, 39
Living Will (Declaration to Physicians), 32
loneliness, 82–83, 90–91
long-term care insurance, 2–3, 20–22, 47–66
   benefits from, receiving, 20, 57–58
   benefits from, tax status of, 54, 57
   caregiving options in, 49–51
   choices/conflicts, 55, 56–57
   choosing a company, 22, 61–63, 64 (chart)
   choosing an agent, 22, 65–66
   contractual provisions of policies, 22, 63
   coverage amount needed, 20–21
   and government benefits, 49
   improvements in, 19–20
   and insurability, 53
   and life expectancy, 47–48
   optional benefits from, 60–61
   premiums for, 20, 56, 58–60, 62
   tax benefits for, 56
   when to buy it, 21–22, 60
   who pays for it, 51–52
   who should buy it, 21–22, 52–56
   who uses it, 21–22, 48

mandatory IRA withdrawal requirements, 15–16
marital deduction trusts, 42–43, 44–45 (charts)
Marital Property Agreement, 38–39
Meals on Wheels, 73
Medicaid, 49
Medicare, 59, 70, 71
mental capacity, 90
millionaires, 50–51
Million Dollar Round Table, 65
Mobile Meals, 73
mobility, 85
money market accounts, 6, 14
Moody's, 64 (chart)

net worth, 9 (illus.), 10
nonprobate transfers of assets, 33, 34, 35–39
nursing homes, 19, 51, 58, 68

"old" (term), 4

paraprofessional aides, 75
partnerships, for property management, 33
payable on death accounts (POD accounts), 37–38
pensions, 12 (illus.)
personal needs chart, 89–92
personal property, 7, 9 (illus.), 10
   and life estate deeds, 36–37
   Marital Property Agreement, 38–39
physical needs, 89–90
POD accounts (payable on death accounts), 37–38
population, aging of, 49, 50 (chart)
portfolio income, 11, 14.
   See also investments

postmortem preferences, 28
Pourover Will, 38–39
power of appointment marital trust, 43
power of attorney
   Durable Power of Attorney,
     23–24, 31
   Healthcare Power of Attorney,
     31–32, 26 (chart) 78
power of withdrawal marital trust, 43
present interest gifts, 40
probate transfers of assets, 33–35
property. *See* personal property
psychological needs, 91

qualified terminable interest property
   trust (QTIP trust), 43

rating services for insurance
   companies, 16, 62–63, 64 (chart)
RCAC (residential care apartment
   complex), 51, 88
remainderman, 36–37
residential care apartment complex
   (RCAC), 51, 88
respite care, 74
retirement, 25. *See also* financial
   planning for retirement; retirement
   communities
retirement communities, 3, 19, 81–104
   activities at, 98–99
   amenities/policies of, 97–98
   community-based residential facility,
     51, 88
   continuing care retirement
     community, 87
   continuum of care in, 87, 95, 101

   dining services at, 99–100
   final decisions about, 102
   financial issues, 86, 92, 101
   first impressions of, 93–94
   and health status, 83–85
   versus home living, 82–86
   housekeeping/laundry services
     at, 100
   housing conditions/options
     in, 95–96
   independent senior living, 87
   intermediate care facility, 88
   lifestyle assessment for, 91–92
   location of, 95
   and loneliness, 82–83, 90–91
   and mobility, 85
   moving to, 102–103
   options in, 86–87
   organizational history/operating
     philosophy of, 94
   personal needs assessment for
     choosing, 89–91
   professional services available in,
     96–97
   questions to ask, 102
   and relationship with management,
     103
   religious services at, 100
   researching a community, 92–93
   residential care apartment complex,
     51, 88
   and safety, 85
   scope of, 87
   skilled nursing facility, 88–89, 96
   and socialization, 85, 90–91
   staffing of, 94–95

and transportation, 98
retirement planning. *See* financial
    planning for retirement
Road Map for Heirs, 26–28

safe environments, 85
senior living.
    See retirement communities
skilled nursing facility (SNF), 88–89, 96
socialization, 85, 90–91
Social Security income, 12 (illus.)
Society of Financial Professionals, 65
Standard & Poor's, 64 (chart)
stocks, 14, 15

talking about issues, 3–4, 23, 105–106
taxes, 15–16
    and capital gains, 11, 39–40
    estate tax, 41–43, 42 (chart),
        44–45 (charts)
    gift tax, 40, 41 (chart)
    high tax bracket, 7
    income tax, 39–40
    and insurance benefits, 54, 56, 57
    and living trusts, 36, 38, 39
    tax-exempt accounts, 7
testamentary trust, 34
transfer on death securities
    (TOD securities), 37–38
trusts
    joint, 43, 44 (chart)
    living, 33, 35–36, 38, 39
    marital deduction, 42–43,
        44–45 (charts)
    revocable, 38, 39, 43, 45 (chart)
    testamentary, 34

ward, definition of, 30
Washington Will, 38
wealth, concentrations of, 50–51
Weiss Ratings, 16
welfare benefits, 49
wills, 2
    and joint/revocable trusts, 43,
        44–45 (charts)
    Pourover Will, 38–39
    and probate assets/intestacy laws, 34
    Washington Will, 38

O R D E R   F O R M

OldTalk New Conversations

A Planning Guide for Seniors and Their Families

To order copies of **OldTalk**, please complete the form below. (Please feel free to duplicate this form.)

I would like to order _____ copies of **OldTalk** at $14.95 per copy (plus postage and handling).

Book Total
  (_____ copies at $14.95 per copy) $_____

Sales Tax
  (Wisconsin Residents add 5.6%) $_____

Shipping and Handling
  ($3.00 for first book; $1.50 for each
  additional book) $_____

Total Amount Enclosed $_____

Checks should be made payable to:
OldTalk LLC. Please do not send cash.

Ordered By:
Name: _____
Address: _____
City: _____
State: _____ Zip: _____
Phone Number: (_____) _____

Ship To (if different from above):
Name: _____
Address: _____
City: _____
State: _____ Zip: _____

Please complete this order form and mail it to:
OldTalk
c/o SelectStaff, Inc.
4433 N. Oakland Ave., Milwaukee, WI 53211